DATE DUE

james dickey:

the expansive imagination

JAMES DICKEY:

THE EXPANSIVE IMAGINATION

A Collection of Critical Essays

edited by **Richard J. Calhoun**

EVERETT / EDWARDS, inc.

POST OFFICE BOX 1060
DELAND, FLORIDA 32720

Standard Book Number: 0-912112-00-X
Library of Congress Catalog Card Number 72-90914
Everett/Edwards, inc., DeLand, Flroida 32720
©1973 by Richard J. Calhoun

Published 1973.
Printed in The United States of America

to Doris, my wife,

to Bob Hill, my colleague in modern poetry,

and to Jim, for writing poetry in the first place

Contents

ABOUT THE EDITOR

Richard J. Calhoun, Alumni Professor of English at Clemson University, received his B.A. from Peabody College, his M.A. from Johns Hopkins and his Ph.D. from the University of North Carolina. He was awarded a postdoctoral fellowship in the COOPERATIVE PROGRAM IN THE HUMANITIES at Duke University and the University of North Carolina. He was a Senior Fulbright Lecturer in American literature in Yugoslavia during 1969-70 and has lectured in Italy for the United States Information Service. His essays have appeared in Warren French's THE TWENTIES: POETRY & PROSE, Everett/Edwards, inc., 1972; and he wrote the bibliography on The Southern Renascence in A BIBLIOGRAPHICAL GUIDE TO THE STUDY OF SOUTHERN LITERATURE, edited by Louis D. Rubin, Jr., LSU Press, 1969. More of Dr. Calhoun's essays have appeared in Southern Review, Southern Literary Journal, South Atlantic Bulletin, Emerson Society Quarterly *and the* South Carolina Review *of which he is assistant editor.*

PREFACE

In 1957 James Dickey was a successful advertising copy writer during the day while trying to begin a career as a poet by writing poetry at night. A decade later, with the appearance of *Poems 1957-1967*, Dickey was recognized as a significant force in American poetry, regarded by some critics as perhaps the nearest rival to Robert Lowell as a major American poet. Today, in the 1970's, he has emerged both as one of the most versatile of American writers—poet, critic, novelist—and as a public personality, if not on the scale of Norman Mailer or Truman Capote, certainly as our most publicly visible poet. For James Dickey has been interviewed and self-interviewed; he has become one of the most successful readers of his own poems on the lecture circuits; like Capote and Mailer, he has increased his public exposure by appearing on television talk shows; and he is the principal author of the script for the movie version of his novel, *Deliverance*, even appearing as an actor in the movie.

Not surprisingly, Dickey's rise to status as a major American poet and to visibility as a literary personality has been so sudden and so phenomenal that his poetry has not received the same attention that the poet has. The only book-length study has been Laurence Lieberman's excellent but slender introduction to a selection of Dickey's poems, *The Achievement of James Dickey*. It is this critical vacuum that the present volume is intended to fill, as the first book-length critical evaluation of Dickey as poet, critic, and novelist.

I think the primary function of the introduction to a volume like this is to comment on what is included and, in the case of an active writer, to update the volume as of the time the collection goes off to press. I have included what I regard as the first major essay on Dickey as a poet, H. L. Weatherby's "The Way of Exchange in James Dickey's Poetry," which identifies a major vehicle used by Dickey in the poems he wrote in the early to mid-1960's—an imaginative and often reciprocal exchange between Dickey and animals, the dead, and primitive natural forces. Peter Davison, in "The Great Grassy World From Both Sides," was the first critic to give Dickey equal status with Robert Lowell, to compare and contrast the themes and styles of these two significant poets, and to predict in some degree the future development of their poetry. Richard Kostelanetz's "Flyswatter and Gadfly" and my own essay, "Whatever Happened to the Poet-Critic?" are attempts to assess Dickey as an important literary critic and to relate his criticism to his poetry. The Carolyn Kizer-James Boatwright interview is the first and still the best attempt to feel out Dickey's own ideas on himself as a poet, and it makes a significant contribution to the development of a legend about Dickey as a virile, woodsy, athletic, folksy Southern poet, who seeks both to celebrate primitive forces in nature and to begin a new cult of virility in modern American literature. Laurence Lieberman's "The Worldly Mystic" updates Weatherby's "The Way of Exchange," describing a dual role of the persona in Dickey's poems—the familiar celebrant of natural forces lost to modern man but, at the same time, a speaker with distinctly mystical yearnings.

Arthur Gregor's "James Dickey: American Romantic" is another poet's attempt to point out the romanticism of Dickey. It is intended, in Gregor's words, to be an appreciation of that aspect of his poetry in order to demonstrate that in his own individualistic way James Dickey "belongs firmly in the tradition of the great romantics from Coleridge to Dylan Thomas and Theodore Roethke." George Lensing's essay, "James Dickey and the Movements of Imagination," is an attempt to relate Dickey to an important aspect of the imaginative projections of American poets in the 1960's, which he and Ronald Moran have described as "the emotive imagination."[1] In Dickey's case the emotive imagination is "empirical reality psychically read through the imagination."

Laurence Lieberman, in "Notes on James Dickey's Style," and Paul Ramsey, in "James Dickey: Meter and Structure," view Dickey's stylistic evolutions from radically different points of view. Professor Ramsey prefers Dickey's earlier end-stopped, rising trimeter to his later freer metrics and verse forms. Expressing a contrary view, Professor Lieberman regards Dickey's split line as "an extremely important development," making it possible for Dickey to move "toward a more direct engagement with life-experience than ever before." William J. Martz and Thomas O. Sloan show Dickey's modernity by focusing on two of his major poems. Martz demonstrates that for a professedly positive poet there is surprisingly a paradox of meaningless being in "Cherrylog Road"; while Sloan, in an important essay, shows that open poems like the "May Day Sermon" achieve "an optimum presentational immediacy" which causes "the reader to forget literary judgments entirely and simply experience." Robert Hill deals with an important but often neglected aspect of Dickey, undoubtedly relevant to the fact that he is a Southern poet—his comic poses.

Finally, Ronald B. Marin, until recently a colleague of Dickey's in creative writing at the University of South

1. Ronald Moran and George Lensing, "The Emotive Imagination: A New Departure in American Poetry," *Southern Review*, III (Winter, 1967), 51-67.

Carolina, attempts to elucidate the thematics of Dickey's best-selling novel, *Deliverance*, and also to relate the themes to those of Dickey's poetry. My own review of *Self-Interviews* and *The Eye-Beaters* serves as an epilogue to the present volume, tracing changes in Dickey's style and themes but also pointing out that there is a thematic continuity with his earlier poetry.

Quite obviously Dickey's critics have not covered every aspect of his poetry; and, although a few of his previous admirers felt that his 1970 volume, *The Eye-Beaters*, represented a decline in the quality of his poetry, his poetic energies are still intact. Consequently, no critical study can quite keep pace. There must always be a critical lag with a poet of such prodigious energies. The present volume should, however, provide an introduction to one of our most significant poets as he enters the decade of the 1970's.

Richard James Calhoun
Clemson University

COPYRIGHTS AND ACKNOWLEDGEMENTS

The editor is grateful to the following publishers and authors for permission to quote from the works named below:

BASIC BOOKS for a passage from "The Poet Turns on Himself," from *Poets On Poetry* edited by Howard Nemerov, copyright © 1969 by Howard Nemerov (Basic Books, Inc.).

PETER DAVISON for "The Great Grassy World From Both Sides," copyright © 1967, 1971 by Peter Davison.

DELACORTE PRESS, for a passage from W. H. Auden, *Nineteenth Century British Minor Poets,* copyright © 1966 by Richard Wilbur.

DEPARTMENT OF SPEECH, COMMUNICATION, AND THEATRE ARTS, University of Minnesota for "The Open Poem Is a Now Poem: Dickey's May Day Sermon," by Thomas O. Sloan, printed in *Literature as Revolt and Revolt as Literature: Three Studies in the Rhetoric of Non-Oratorical Forms.* The Proceedings of the Fourth Annual University of Minnesota Spring Symposium in Speech Communication. Minneapolis, Minnesota, May 3, 1969, pp. 17-31.

DOUBLEDAY & COMPANY, INC. for passages from *The Eye-Beaters, Blood, Victory, Madness, Buckhead, and Mercy* by James Dickey, copyright © 1968, 1969, 1970 by James

THE SEWANEE REVIEW for "The Way of Exchange in James Dickey's Poetry," by H. L. Weatherby from *The Sewanee Review,* LXXIV, 3 (Summer 1966), copyright © 1966 by the University of the South, reprinted by permission of the author and the publisher.

THE SHENANDOAH for "A Conversation with James Dickey," by Carolyn Kizer and James Boatwright from *The Shenandoah: The Washington and Lee University Review,* XVIII, 1 (Autumn 1966).

THE SOUTH CAROLINA REVIEW for " 'His Reason Argues with His Invention'—James Dickey's *Self-Interviews* and *The Eye-Beaters,* " by Richard J. Calhoun from *The South Carolina Review,* III, 2 (June 1971).

THE SOUTH CAROLINA REVIEW for "James B. Dickey's *Deliverance:* Darkness Visible," by Daniel B. Marin from *The South Carolina Review,* III, 1 (November 1970).

THE SOUTHERN LITERARY JOURNAL for "Whatever Happened to the Poet-Critic?" by Richard J. Calhoun from *The Southern Literary Journal,* I, 1 (Autumn 1968).

WESLEYAN UNIVERSITY PRESS for *Poems 1957-1967* by James Dickey. Poems from which passages are quoted are copyright by James Dickey and included in his *Poems 1957-1967.* The passages are reprinted by permission of Wesleyan University Press, publisher.

Chapter I

A CONVERSATION WITH JAMES DICKEY

I asked Carolyn Kizer to interview James Dickey because I knew she was a good friend of his, their friendship dating from before the time when Carolyn was at the University of Washington editing Poetry Northwest *and Jim was teaching at Reed College in Portland, Oregon.*

Carolyn suggested that I help out with the interview, which I did by supplying the tape recorder and one or two questions. The meeting took place on a warm, sunny Sunday afternoon in late August, in Carolyn's house in Georgetown. Both poets had moved east: Carolyn to serve as Director of Literary Programs for the National Endowment for the Arts, Jim to assume his duties as Consultant in Poetry at the Library of Congress. He had driven in from his home in Leesburg, Virginia, accompanied by his teenage son. They were late, Jim explained, because a gang of motorcyclists looking suspiciously like Hell's Angels had roared up in their neighborhood as they were preparing to leave.

After Carolyn had fortified us with a drink, the three of us gathered around the recorder. Carolyn announced that she would begin somewhat abrasively, in hopes that Jim's first response would be a lively one.

Reprinted by permission from *The Shenandoah*, Vol. XVIII, No. 1 (Autumn, 1966).

KIZER

Sometimes I have an uncomfortable feeling when I read articles by you and about you and the jacket blurbs on your books, some of which I suspect were written by you, about this persona that you're foisting off on the American public—you know, Dickey the great hero of the virility cult, great sportsman, gamesman, football player, ex-war ace—I mean all these things which are true but which seem to me not as relevant to you or your poetry as perhaps you'd like the rest of us to believe. I mean, how much of this is "con" and how much of it is real?

DICKEY

It would be hard to say. It wouldn't be true to say that I have no interest in people knowing about these things in regard to me. I do. But they are not in any sense any kind of substitute for anything that I have written. I was not published at the beginning, I suppose not now either, because of playing football at Clemson or basketball there or any other things that I have done. Those things have come up, and other people have noticed them and made something out of them. But this just happens to be the way my life ran. And this business about the virility cult: that's something that delights me. I'd love to believe it. If a Dickey virility cult grew up that would be fine with me! But this has nothing to do with what I'm trying to put down on a page.

KIZER

No, I realize that. But what I'm talking about, Jim, is whether you have deliberately tried to construct a persona to stand between you the poet and, I think, the extraordinarily sensitive human being, in the interests of protecting yourself from what's becoming a rather large following.

DICKEY

No, I don't think so. What you do deliberately and what you do inadvertently are sort of hard to distinguish between sometimes. America has always taken up its writers and made them cult figures of some kind or another. But I don't look on myself as a kind of poetical Hemingway.

KIZER

Oh, not at all. I realize you don't. But what I'm wondering is if you want the outside world to look on you that way to protect the sensitive you that doesn't want to be a cult figure.

DICKEY

I have never had any such conscious intention as that. American writers have always had to come up with some kind of strategy to protect their delicate inner workings and so on: I realize that this is true. But I have never had any feeling that this is so in my case. If people want to pick up on these things and make something out of them it's very good for my ego. I'm delighted. But it's not a strategy which enables me to work when otherwise I wouldn't be able to work. Not at all. I don't look on myself as having a kind of schizophrenic existence or trying to come up with one. First an existence as a man and a guy who likes to do certain things, who likes to hunt animals and swim and do various other things of that sort and then another kind of shy, sensitive plant who writes poems and has to be protected by this other sort of Hemingway type. No, no. It's all just part of the same existence. I don't have any great feeling of distinction between doing one thing or another except as far as techniques are concerned. There's not a whole lot of difference to me between playing a guitar and shooting a bow. Just a difference of technique. Or writing a poem. It's a feeling of satisfaction that you get out of all three sort of equally. And they complement each other in a way. What you want to do is keep the self whole. I don't like this business of setting poetry off into a separate compartment that's got to have all this array and battery of protective devices to enable it to exist at all. I don't feel this. Maybe it would be necessary for other people but I have never felt any such necessity myself.

KIZER

I'll always remember the first time I met you when we bumped into each other in the Gotham Book Mart. I remember one of the first speeches you ever made to me. You thought writers in this country were far, far too self-protective. They were scared to work at ordinary jobs or scared to work in advertising agencies and the like. They were always afraid of intellectual rape. I remember your saying to me then that you weren't the least bit afraid, and you thought writers would be a lot better off if they were tougher about things like that.

DICKEY

I sure do think so. I've always disliked this business of the writer, especially the poet, being a rare soul who is misunderstood by everybody around him and who takes to having all these very secret private rituals and so on. Rilke is an example of this. He is a very great poet but is also the kind of human being that I absolutely abhor.

KIZER

Well, we all know who the delicate little flower poets are—you know, people like Ben Jonson, and Francois Villon.

DICKEY

Oh, those are the delicate flowers that I like best.

BOATWRIGHT

What about the universities and the fact that universities take over poets? Will this inevitably make poetry that much more academic?

DICKEY

Well, it will in a way. Again it depends so much on the person. People talk about academic poets—these naive, simple-minded people like Kenneth Rexroth—always drawing lines of demarcation which have *less* than zero value. Over here are academic poets and over here are such and such poets. Virile beatnik poets, you know. That sort of thing.

KIZER

And the virile, beatnik poets who are talking about academic poets are always trying to get their jobs when they hear that one of them is sick or going to Europe, or something.

DICKEY

Well, quite a lot of the so-called beat poets are in universities and glad to be there.

KIZER

Exactly. But a lot of it, whether the academies are going to do anybody any harm or the business world or anything else, depends on how *formed* one is.

DICKEY

It depends on oneself and one's own resources. And also, it depends on how one takes one's own writing. I think one of the main difficulties in the life of the modern poet is getting time to work. It seems to me that one ought to be prepared to go quite a long way with any agency which gives one *that*. That's the simple and absolutely indispensable prerequisite for any writer: time to sit down and work out his problems on the page. This the university does provide. Now what it doesn't provide—and this is a much more intangible but also very necessary ingredient—is some kind of working arrangement whereby the writer can experience the world pretty much in the way he feels he needs to. This is where the university is sometimes difficult to reconcile with one's own ambitions and works. If you have a distinct taste for low life, as I do—the "wild side of life," as the old juke box tune has it—the university can be a pretty sticky situation. You're not supposed to be like that when you're teaching the young. But if there's something in your being that needs to *be* like that at certain times you ought to be able to do it. And this is where the university is a blockage.

KIZER

It seems to me though that one of the crucial things here is that we may have an instinct for variety—for living one kind of life one year and another kind the next. And the academy tends to . . . .

DICKEY

Well, it doesn't absolutely negate it or make it impossible but it surely makes it difficult—at times. This is when you do have to resort to a certain amount of subterfuge. If you want to go down in some low dive and get drunk, you don't do it as Professor X. You do it as a "guy." Then you put on your California-type dark glasses and . . . (I've never done this but I can imagine that it might be necessary).

KIZER

I know various poets who've got into a lot of trouble because they didn't do it. But also, your academic career has been one which has invited a lot of changes. I mean, you've moved on from university to university, college to college.

DICKEY

I hit the universities like a thief. I have a horror of getting committed to one. And yet, eventually I want to settle down.

KIZER

But as Vachel Lindsay used to say, he had a horror of digging in. And I think this is what the academy encourages us to do.

DICKEY

It does. There's this kind of myth of stability and what's the word—"security"—and maturity. Any time I hear somebody say to somebody else that he is immature or that he should become mature my sympathies go out immediately to the one who is being told to be mature.

KIZER

Don't you think that on the whole poets tend to be rather emotionally retarded? It takes them a long time to grow up emotionally, if ever.

DICKEY

Well, again, I distrust myself. This business of growing up emotionally is so many times taken to mean simply conformity or feeling what one is supposed to feel as opposed to what one really does feel.

KIZER

I want to be good to other people, I want to be *that* mature, but I don't want the kind of stability, the kind of maturity, that we've been talking about.

DICKEY

I think the only good state of mind for a poet is the feeling of perpetual possibility. That something that happens today or might happen tomorrow is going to have a very powerful effect and a very great deal of value for you. If you know pretty much what's going to happen from day to day and you know the value or lack of value that it's had before, it's not likely to have any more than that tomorrow. It's this business of the unknown that seems to me to be the most fertile ground for the poet to live in. The thing that might happen that is totally unforeseen. Almost everything that I've ever written comes out of things that have happened to me by chance. There's got to be a way for the poet to open the world up to himself from the standpoint of there being an infinite number of chances, none of which he can predict, for him to move through and among.

BOATWRIGHT

You say poet. But since you talked about poetry as being a part of the whole man . . . .

DICKEY

No, I think the same thing would be true of any man. He doesn't have to be a poet. Or a poet *especially*. But a poet is not anything more or less than an intensifed man anyway.

KIZER

But this means accepting a great deal of permanent insecurity, doesn't it?

DICKEY

Yes it does. But that seems to me a magnificently healthy environment for the soul or the spirit, or whatever you'd want to call it.

KIZER

I agree. But it's just exactly what most people aren't willing to accept.

DICKEY

That's right. But now this business of security. One of the things that I dislike most of all is to open up a magazine and see a long, sententious advertisement for an insurance company. Now the insurance companies and their agents are the most subversive of all people on earth. And they show off a nice looking old guy and nice looking old lady but the immediate feeling you have is well, they'd probably be having a good time if they weren't so old. It's like advertisements for glasses ostensibly showing that glasses don't make a pretty girl any less attractive or maybe they make her more attractive. But my feeling is that, gee, wouldn't she be pretty if she wasn't wearing glasses.

KIZER

There is a girl in my office, a pretty blonde girl, who says, "You know, in twenty-three years I can retire from the federal government and I'm going to open a card shop in Pasadena." Now what could be more horrible?

DICKEY

There's a sad possibility that it might also be wonderful.

KIZER

But very remote.

DICKEY

It wouldn't be right for me or you.

KIZER

Of course security is an illusion. I mean, we're all going to die.

DICKEY

That's right. Now money is going to help you do some things. There's no doubt about it. I was born poor. I don't like to be a poor person. But money is good only as it realizes more life for you and more possibilities. More intensification of experience, more variety and so on, instead of the dull kind of deadening treadmill of routine that so many people are bogged down on from the time they get into their teens until the time they die. I worked in business for five or six years and the thing that I detested about it was the deadening effect of it. And the fact that you are continually eaten up and your emotional strength depleted by problems which in reality you have not the slightest interest in.

KIZER

And which really don't exist, in our terms.

DICKEY

But on which you are dependent for your livelihood and the livelihood of your family and children. This is a savagely destructive way to live a human life. Savagely destructive and obscene, it seems to me.

KIZER

You always have talked and always will, I hope, about its being the whole person out of which poetry is written. And I wish you would say something about the body, about the physical aspect of this wholeness, because I think you're unique in this. Most poets are, you know, slobs. They're overweight or they have indoor pallor, they don't take care of themselves, they're covered with cigarette ash. But you do have some sense of your own body and of the necessity of taking care of it. And this has some relevance to the poetry too, does it not?

DICKEY

A very great deal. I suppose that I'm not overly stupid, although I run into, every day, people that are a lot smarter than I am. My work is almost entirely physical rather than intellectual or mental. There are many times when I am trying to write something that reason tells me to say in a certain way but it just doesn't *feel* right. It's something in the region of the solar plexus which tells me to say it this other way. There's no reason to say it the other way except that I just *like* it better. There's a very real connection of the whole physiological complex with what the poem is trying to say. I can feel it. It's instinctual with me and I would say largely visceral and muscular. There's a very real involvement of the musculature, such as it is, in the act. I like that. Terribly intellectual people like Auden and Eliot, essentially indoor men, probably would put this down as nonsense and they could easily prove me wrong. But I wouldn't go along with any such proof because I *know* and I know that I know. There is an old saying that the fox knows many things, but the hedgehog knows one *big* thing. I know one big thing. I think I do.

BOATWRIGHT

What's the connection between that and what you have said elsewhere about the uneducated or the self-educated poet? What's the connection between a poet's knowing something about poetry or tradition or history and his need to be physical, visceral?

DICKEY

I think it's a different kind of knowing. Again, I'm a little fearful about talking too much about this kind of thing. I can't intellectualize about this to any enlightening degree. I never have been able to do it for myself. And there's no reason to suppose that I would be able to do it for you, either. But again, all the different men that a man is split up into and which one must constantly try to bring into one's own kind of whole man who is really better than he is—you've got a lot of different sides that you do need to reconcile and yet they seem to exist coterminously, at your best moments, and in perfect accord. I've got a side that had rather do nothing than sit down and read long essays, critical essays, and argue with the author over every sentence. I enjoy that very much. But when I'm trying to write something, the best thing that I can do is to get into some kind of state in which no poem ever was written before: to believe what I'm trying to do is the first attempt that has ever been made to say this. I'm awfully tired of the English poetic tradition and of the awful kind of dead hand that Eliot insists has to be clamped on the individual talent by the poetic tradition. I don't think any of that's necessary. You can use something from it every now and then for your own purposes but the main emphasis to me is not tradition and the individual talent but tradition (small letters) and the individual talent (large letters), which may or may not have anything very much to do with the tradition. In fact, in some cases, in the ultimate case of the "new man," the new great poet, who I hope some day will arise, it will have nothing whatever to do with the tradition except insofar as the poet uses the English language.

KIZER

Well, perhaps you and I would say—we would have the emphasis put on tradition as it can assist the individual talent.

DICKEY

I agree. Or the tradition as being entirely irrelevant to the talent. It might be useful but it's not as Eliot says: a body of law that's got to be considered all the time. I don't believe that at all. I have read for years all these, well, translations when I didn't know the language, which I almost never did, but I've tried to come into conjunction in one way or another with Eskimo dance rituals and Bantu hunting songs and that sort of thing. And the revelations of those so-called folk as far as poetic imagery is considered are marvelously rich and evocative. They have nothing to do with Alexander Pope's use of the heroic couplet or Wordsworth's use of

Milton's blank verse or any of that sort of thing. They never
knew of the existence of it, to begin with. And yet those
people are saying something out of a condition with which
they are in a precarious and dangerous and sometimes
desperate harmony, but always a harmony of some kind
which, even when the environment destroys them is some
kind of harmony with the environment. I'm looking for some
way to *relate* to things again and this is the reason I dislike so
much these poets of alienation who feel humiliated by
everything and who are endlessly examining their own
motives. I'm looking for a way to respond with one hundred
per cent of my humanity and not respond with ten per cent
while ninety per cent stands back and says, Dickey you really
are in love with your mother when you like this flower. I'm
not putting down psychoanalysis or anything like that. I'm
only trying to get some kind of way to give absolute,
wholehearted response. Somebody (I think it was Yeats
maybe) said that a man running at full speed has neither a
brain nor a heart. I'm trying to get into the psychological
state of the man running at full speed and see what he does
have.

KIZER

Another thing that I resent, though, about the use that
Auden and Eliot make of the word tradition is that it's such
an exclusive, countryclub interpretation of the word tradition. You just mentioned Eskimo culture, etc. I mean "tradition" is always Wasp tradition isn't it? It's western Euro-
pean tradition. Whose tradition, and whose individual talent?
It's a broader subject than they dream of in their philosophy.

DICKEY

I want to find some way in which it will be profitable to
cut loose and go all out in some way, poetically, rather than

constantly being under wraps and held back and hag-ridden by doubts. I want to find some way to commit absolutely and utterly to the poem that I'm trying to write. Now this may be romantic. Again, it can be disproved. I can disprove it myself and I will say that a good deal of what I am saying is nonsense. And yet there is a feeling I have that I want to try to do this and I will stake anything that I need to up to my life on being able to do it.

KIZER

I feel that a part of your detestation for this kind of fashionable masochism and *mea culpa* intellectualism that is all around us these days is simply because it's non-functional. It doesn't do anything for a poet or a creative person to go around beating his breast and wailing except to give him an assortment of hang-ups that he doesn't need.

DICKEY

Well, somebody may need 'em, but I don't need 'em.

BOATWRIGHT

You mentioned that the only tradition is the tradition of the English language. So you're not joining the group which talks about an American language as distinct from an English language.

DICKEY

I don't know that much about it. There obviously are differences but basically it's English with sub-varieties and variations which depend on our living over here and their living over there. But it's basically English, it's American language English language, or the American version of the English language.

KIZER

Well, again it's rather irrelevant. You don't have to accept your mother at the expense of your grandmother. You can accept them both.

DICKEY

Local differences do matter. There are lots of magnificent Americanisms we have because we are Americans and our history has been what it has been. As well as a lot of magnificent Englishisms that they have because theirs has been as it has been.

BOATWRIGHT

But you don't feel that you've got to search out an American idiom?

DICKEY

No. Do you mean like Kenneth Fearing used to do, maybe? A lot of slang and idiomatic things? No. In fact I sort of stay away from that. I wouldn't use it well. I know. There are certain things that I stay away from because I know that I have no ability to work in that genre. Satire is one.

BOATWRIGHT

I was going to ask you about that.

DICKEY

I haven't any desire or any ability to write satirical works. I can say mean things about people but I can't make them funny.

KIZER

Anyway, it's better to do it in private life.

BOATWRIGHT

I was struck in reading about the National Book Awards by the presence of two Southerners: there you were and there was Katherine Anne Porter, and then the piece in *Life* says that you are not a "Southern" poet. What do you feel about the Southern writer's being so obviously more important than he ought to be, if you consider the region, the number of people in the region, and so on?

DICKEY

I have one central feeling about the South and myself and that is the best thing that ever happened to me was to have been born a Southerner. First as a man and then as a writer. And yet I would not under any circumstances want to feel that I was limited in any way by being a Southerner, that I was expected, say, by other people to indulge in the kind of regional chauvinism that has sometimes been indulged in by Southern writers. One has a history which is intimately in one way or another bound up with the history of one's own people and one's own ancestors and people who live in the same region one does. The South has a tragic history, as everybody knows, but it has given me as a human being a set of values, some of which are deplorable, obviously, but also some of which are the best things that I have ever had as a human being. It's like in the E. M. Forster novel where Forster says of Mrs. Wilcox—"she let her ancestors help her." This is something that I feel very strongly. I have only run-of-the-mill ancestors but they knew that one was supposed to do certain things. Even the sense of evil, which is very strong with me, would not exist if I had no sense of what evil was.

KIZER

I remember Mr. Ransom saying once that a sense of evil was absolutely *essential* to poetry.

DICKEY

I agree with that.

KIZER

And he said the trouble with somebody like Wordsworth was that he didn't have it. And that you've got to be wrestling with this all the time in poetry.

DICKEY

And somebody like Baudelaire capitulated to evil so much that it became a kind of Puritanism in itself.

KIZER

But in another sense he lost the other end of the dialectic.

DICKEY

That's right.

KIZER

You have to keep the tension between the two, as Stanley Kunitz says.

DICKEY

This is more or less, I think, the case. But again you don't keep it because it's going to produce valuable poems. This is an attitude that I just detest. These people who are saving themselves for posterity. My God, a poem is not anything but some words on a page. In the eternal battle between life and poetry or life and art, I'll take life. And if poetry were not a kind of means, in my case, of intensifying experience and of giving a kind of personal value to it I would not have any interest in it whatever.

KIZER

That's very interesting. Because I was going to begin this interview by saying that in some ways you're becoming to me a kind of Byronic figure and that's such a Byronic statement: if I have to choose between art and life I'll take life. I wonder if you've ever felt any sense of identity with Byron . . . .

DICKEY

As a matter of fact, he's the first poet I ever read except under duress. I don't like him very much as a poet, but . . .

KIZER

Well, that's irrelevant to what I'm concerned with.

DICKEY

But the figure of Byron, this is valuable to me. He is the example of the kind of man that I've always attached a particular kind of personal value to. The guy who is an enormous phony, but who makes the public take him on his own terms, the terms of his persona. And underneath it all is an extremely practical, hardheaded, and utterly honest person.

KIZER

It seems to me clear that Byron would have been a better poet if he had been a little less interested in the living Byron and a little more interested in the poetry that he was going to leave behind him. He really didn't give all that much of a damn, did he?

DICKEY

I'm not sure that's so. Byron never exhibited the slightest capacity to be a poet in any sense that I would think of as being a poet. He's an amusing social satirist who has a good many affinities with somebody like Auden in our time. I've never cared for that at all.

KIZER

I'm just interested in the Byron that wrote *Don Juan*.

DICKEY

Well, this is the social commentary.

KIZER

But don't you feel that he was trying harder?

DICKEY

Well, he was, but again that's a genre that doesn't attract me very much.

KIZER

But that's not where the parallels occur: the thing that we have said is that to him his life was more important than his art in the sense he made his art serve his life, and in the case of his relations with ladies sometimes it was quite useful to him in that way. Secondly, perhaps the only fault that I think of you as having as a poet is occasionally being rather self-indulgent. Sometimes the poems are longer, looser, and you're letting yourself out a bit more than I think . . . But perhaps one reason you're doing this, and that may be the reason Byron did it—you don't want to interrupt the flow, you want to get it out. Why, do you know?

DICKEY

Well, because in my own case (I can't speak for anybody else) when the impulse comes it brings with it almost everything that is necessary to the poem and also a lot of things that are not necessary to the poem. And sometimes it takes a while to figure out which is which. If you sort it out as you go along you're just as likely to cut out the good as you are the bad. In fact, *more* likely. You can always take out. But you can't always put in. At least *I* can't.

KIZER

Do you have much angst about the flow ceasing? I mean do you have a sense of having to write now while you're doing it well, having to write *now* . . . .

DICKEY

Well, a little of that. I thought you meant ceasing permanently.

KIZER

Oh no, no. I mean that you're riding a marvelous wave now of creativity . . . .

DICKEY

Oh yes. I want to go with that.

KIZER

You're riding with it.

DICKEY

I'm always anxious to cast myself on that particular flood.

KIZER

I believe with Yeats that the sorting out can always take place later. We can go back and revise it when we're sixty.

DICKEY

But if you write it one line at a time and sort of choke up and if you're unable to go farther because this line is not very good . . .

KIZER

Or if a critical censorship takes place too soon . . .

DICKEY

Yes. If the critic is nagging you all the time you are not going to get anything out of your muse because he'll just flap away. I love the sense of the whole thing coming—good, bad and indifferent—everything coming and coming and coming. That's a marvelous feeling. That's the best part of writing poetry, to me. Because in this particular part you have enough good things that you're getting down that you're having a marvelous exalted sense of absolute possibilities. You know, you think, Jesus, this came to me, this phrase, and if I can get a lot of other ones that are as good as this, this is going to be the greatest poem ever written! But at that stage of things the phrase is buried in the poem with a lot of things that are pretty good and some that are bad. But the eternal hope of a poet is that you seize on those good fragments and you say, boy, I'm going to make the whole thing like *that* phrase! So through the next successive stages you try to do that.

KIZER

But in the end of this rush and flow, and at the end of these phrases is death. Would you agree with or perhaps care to enlarge on something that Dick Hugo said once that I thought was very interesting. When somebody asked him what was the difference between poets and other people he said, well, he thought poets thought about death *all the time*.

DICKEY

Well, I know I do. But I wouldn't claim that as any exclusive prerogative.

KIZER

No, but I think it's amazing that most people don't. I mean the kind of things we were talking about, insurance company advertisements about old age, and security, and so on. This is the great unsaid thing. When you get there, my friend, you're going to be dead very soon.

DICKEY

I was reading something of John Fowles—a tendentious book of aphorisms somebody sent me—but one thing interested me. He said, death is nothing without you and you are nothing without it. I know I'm nothing without it, but the notion that death is nothing without me is something that sort of interested me.

KIZER

We can use that. Do you have a sense of working against time and how urgent . . .

DICKEY

But that can be a very constricting thing. It can make you work on poems simply because time is growing less and you feel that you ought to be working on *some* poem. So you work on *some* poem. But for me there's got to be the sense of the absolute necessity of this particular thing that I'm trying to write. I don't want to be a professional poet in the sense of sitting down and doing something in verse every day. If I can't preserve the sense of personal excitement that I get from it, I have no interest in working on it.

KIZER

Don't you also feel in a curious way that death is further away in one's early forties than in one's late twenties?

DICKEY

Well, in a way.

KIZER

I mean death has retreated in my life.

DICKEY

You spoke about angst and there's a peculiar conjunction of kinds of angst in this particular situation, at least for me. The feeling that I have, the better I'm working, the more aware of my own death I am. That when I've got a great flow going it would be doubly sad to lose it now. When I'm just slopping around the house, drinking, and not trying to write anything, not even answering correspondence, I say well, I've already done a lot of work, I've got five books of poems out, and I'll stand on this, and if I died now it would just do nothing but relieve me of a lot of boredom. But when I'm really working good, I don't want to die. There is a kind of conjunction between work and the way one feels about existence. I suppose. At least so it is with me.

KIZER

I would like to go back and pick up something else that we were talking about a while ago. It relates to the topic of death. And that is, of aging. You were talking about how, well perhaps dependent isn't the right word, *concerned* you are with physicality, with the physical in your poetry and of course also with sexuality. I sometimes have extreme anxiety about what I'm going to write about as I go on getting older because I feel this way about my poetry. That it's very dependent on physicality and sexuality; and if this goes what's going to take its place? What are your feelings about this?

DICKEY

I plan to go on in the sexuality field as long as I can.

KIZER

But biological processes are going to intervene. We can go through the Yeats bit and all that and have goat glands but I mean—inevitably it's going to catch up with us before we feel that we are finished with our working life, and then what?

DICKEY

Well, I don't know. . . . There's supposed to be a kind of serenity that sets in with old intellectual. . .

KIZER

That's not going to do much for poetry, Baby. I mean. . . .

DICKEY

I don't know. You take each age as it comes. If I could get some kind of transcendental serenity and magnificence of vision out of an absolutely sexless state I would want the utmost intensification of that, too.

KIZER

But Yeats got transcendental serenity out of goat glands. . . .

DICKEY

If somebody demonstrated to me that they would work, or if I had the money to pay for it . . . !

KIZER

The point is, you are peculiarly related to this whole subject. There are poets, the gamesmen, the game players, . . . sex doesn't matter much to them or, you know, the sort of polite lady poets who want you to know they went to Italy last summer, the place-droppers. I mean, this doesn't bother them . . .

DICKEY

I just happened to read in the newspaper something that John Masefield, of all people, said, who must be about three hundred years old. Because he's been poet laureate for at least two hundred! And somebody asked him how he felt about being of advanced age and he said, "How magnificent the vision grows at the end." For that reason, I would read anything he ever wrote.

BOATWRIGHT

What about the late poems of Lawrence where he speaks of the dark voyage?

DICKEY

But Lawrence died as a comparatively young man. He was my age. There must be another kind of way to die when you are very, very old. I have diabetes. As a matter of fact, when the doctor told me I had it I said is this going to shorten my life? And he said you should live out your expected time of sixty-eight years. But there ought to be something that corresponds in that period to sexuality or the old kind of "Chinese sage" serenity. There's something in the sixty-eight range of actuarial tables that ought to be good, too, and I intend to find out what it is.

KIZER

Well let *me* know. You may phone me collect, or cable. I think the Chinese did have something there. I think one of the things that they had, and it's very important to me, viz a viz you and other people who write poetry: it's friendship. And it's something that we have to hang on to very hard as poets and as people because it's something that's being bulldozed out of our life like trees and like buildings by this terrible trend toward homogeneity of everything. And yet it is extraordinary poetry in which you sense this feeling that the relations, the non-sexual relations between people could be so desperately important.

DICKEY

I don't know much about Chinese poetry, but desperation seems to be singularly absent from what I have read of it. There's a lot of resigned sadness and so on ... but desperation ...

KIZER

No, desperation as a feeling doesn't exist, but friendship is an area of relationship that it seems to me Western life is losing. That an aspect of human relationship is atrophying in a funny kind of way. Sometimes I have a nightmare that nobody believes in falling in love anymore.

DICKEY

I like that a lot. I like falling in love. In fact, I do it all the time.

KIZER

I think it's terribly important.

DICKEY

It sure is to me.

KIZER

But do you ever have this feeling? That in America

everybody is ceasing to believe in love, particularly in New York City?

DICKEY

Well I'll tell you. There's a kind of a dry rot of cynicism that I've been doing my best to avoid. If I can avoid that and avoid encouraging it in my children I would feel like I had done at least a little something. It's easy and frequently rather cheap to look cynically at almost anything, everything. As Robert Penn Warren says somewhere, when some learned fellow tells him that "Jesus in Gethsemane was only sweating from TB/*Timor mortis conturbat me!*" It's possible to look cynically on anything and everything. We belong to what I guess you could call, for want of a better term, I'm sure there *is* a better term, the "aw, come off it" generation. But I don't want to come off it. I want to get on it.

KIZER

Right! But the point, again, and this is the thing that has always bored me about a lot of the talk of fashionable French intellectuals, the Simone de Beauvoir, Gide group: they've got it all figured out and they've got this cynical attitude towards everything. Madame de Beauvoir wrote in *The Mandarins* about the woman protagonist, like herself, serving her sixteen-year-old daughter and her lover breakfast in bed and thinking that's terribly cool, you know. I think it was an invasion of their privacy, among other things. But the thing I really hate about it is the implication that everything is acceptable, everything is mechanistic, none of it matters very much, it can all be reduced down to a biological level, a mechanical order, a boring mechanical order, and I can't bear any of this. . . .

DICKEY

I agree with you. All of human life, Carolyn, it seems to me, hinges on what you attach value to. It doesn't matter so much *why* you attach value to certain things or any analytical propensities of that sort. But if you see value in things and naturally gravitate towards those things and cultivate them and care for them and live in and about and with them you have the nearest thing that we human beings are ever going to get to a satisfactory life. It doesn't have to be satisfactory to anybody but you. I remember something I read in Patrice de la Tour du Pin's *La Somme de la Poésie*, part of which is a kind of a dialogue where this guy is a kind of cynical Parisian and he systematically goes around milking his glands with various women and sitting in the park reflecting on the futility of everything and the guy who's talking to him says, "Well, you talk about what a desert life is, and surely it is. But would it be so if you were not killing off everything in it?"

KIZER

Exactly, exactly. Being your own flame thrower and destroying everything in front of you. This is the thing that frightens me about fashionable New York and French intellectuals of a certain kind: that the beliefs which they hold about life are destructive to their own art. Therefore, obviously, on the simplest pragmatic level they ought to be thrown out. Because they don't work. They are miserable people and they produce art of a very limited range.

DICKEY

I don't want anybody telling me that the only fashionability as a writer is to be miserable. I've been miserable enough in my time. But it's like Roethke said somewhere toward the end of his life: "In spite of everything I seek to establish some kind of condition of joy." Because I am that way essentially myself, and I mean *essentially*. That may sound sententious, but it is something that I do very profoundly feel. Joy, by God! This is something I'm always . . . I haven't had it but a few times but I'm willing to wait for it to come again. And nobody is going to tell me that it's square to put any faith in this sort of thing. Because it's the only thing that makes existence worth anything at all to me.

KIZER

As Ted said in a very late poem, the right thing happens to the happy man.

DICKEY

Right things *do* happen to the happy man.

KIZER

And we have to have that beautiful receptivity to . . .

DICKEY

Or the great phrase of Henry James—accessibility to experience: to go toward it, hoping that it's going to be good or great. The psychological state with which one greets what comes to one is of absolute importance. If one is determined to be cynical, nothing is going to be good. I'll tell you what I dislike so much: the people who, to give themselves a certain facile superiority, sort of agree with themselves and their compatriots in this opinion. The idea that *everything* is in some way sort of contemptible. Mary McCarthy is this way. If somebody has a nice looking hat on, if a girl or woman has a nice looking hat on at a party, to Mary McCarthy there is something contemptible about its being nice looking. Even if somebody is absolutely pure and good, terms one expects to hear from the nineteenth century, even this is a little bit square. It's naive and a little bit pitiful.

KIZER

Oh, absolutely. I've been called down by glossy intellectuals for using the word "good." In *any* sense. Whether it refers to food or morals. I mean, the term is just not acceptable because it offends their passion for relativism.

DICKEY

I don't want to put Mary McCarthy down. She's a very bright gal. But the single test of whether anybody is valuable to you as a writer is to ask yourself if that writer, Mary McCarthy or whoever else it might be, has or is anything that I'd want to be. Or want to have. And in this case I don't. I would rather have what Roethke has a hundred thousand times more than what Mary McCarthy has. I would rather have what James Agee had than a thousand Mary McCarthys. Now Mary McCarthy could use James Agee in a novel as a figure of the terribly earnest, over-emotional person who really is not aware of the way things really are. But that wouldn't matter to me. He's great.

BOATWRIGHT

Well, isn't there a real return to an acceptance of these square abstractions? The kind of abstractions that Hemingway's characters hated: duty and honor and courage and such words as that. What has returned is a willingness to admit the validity of words like *joy*.

DICKEY

I agree. What we want, again, is to achieve a kind of state in which we can function in the world, not only barely making it, the debits and the credits sort of balancing out so that we can just barely hang in there, but to burst through to some magnificent region of the human personality and the creative mind which will no longer have any debits but which will be all positive: which will be beyond anything that has been yet. I think, again, when we talk about tradition in poetry and all this, I think we've been hung up on a set of middling assumptions which do not have to exist. And once having been destroyed it will be seen as a set of the most trifling and inessential irrelevancies that could possibly be. But if we can unite the joyous man and the absolutely uninhibited imagination we will have done something for our generation, I think.

Chapter II

THE GREAT GRASSY WORLD FROM BOTH SIDES*
The Poetry of Robert Lowell and James Dickey
by Peter Davison

Americans are haunted by the dream of landing on an inhospitable coast, settling along the shore, looking westward into a vast hostile continent and backward over the shoulder to a bleak but necessary sea. The cities of the Old World (Sodom, Rome, London, and the constellations of guilt and terror that were Africa) always lay to the East. Even now our Westerners speak of The East with more wariness than of other points of the compass.

The openness of the American spirit, on the other hand, has always been sought in the opposite direction ("to the land vaguely realizing westward," as Frost had it), though our standards and our limitations come to us as the legacy of the Old World. ("Have the elder races halted?" Walt Whitman asked. "Do they droop and end their lesson, wearied over there beyond the seas? / We take up the task eternal, and the burden, and the lesson / Pioneers! O Pioneers!")

*Adapted from "The Difficulties of Being Major," *Atlantic Monthly*, October 1967. © 1967 by The Atlantic Monthly Company, copyright assigned to Peter Davison 3/11/69. Not registered.

The sea behind us has served in the office of a moat, but, more importantly, as our "connection" (the unconscious meanings are resonant) with the "mother country." Of course we transformed what we inherited. Look at the difference, for example, between the roles played by the sea in British and American legend and language. Over here our pirates were cowboys; our rebellious youths ran away to the Sea of Grass; and the only American maritime adventurers who stirred our imagination were whalers and the clipper-shipmen of the China Trade, pressing on toward the setting sun.

With this continent at our face and that ocean at our back, we were from the beginnings of our national identity overwhelmed by the very scale of our situation, and preoccupied with a massiveness that has pervaded most of our literary aspirations. The Revolution was greeted with an infestation of epic poetry, unread and unreadable; the first flowering of our fiction produced demands for The Great American Novel; American criticism could not come of age in its own eyes until our scholars had elected a pantheon of Major American Writers and hoisted them into position to dominate the new courses and textbooks in American Literature. Since 1945 the demand for major writers has increased until every publishing season critics pick over each crop with the concentration of cannery workers grading fruit.

Not that the insistence on being major has much real meaning unless you are in search of a Goethe or a Dante. Yet it has affected American writers' notions of themselves and thus of the way they write. The career of Norman Mailer has been, both in his own eyes and those of his readers, a series of lunges after Major Status. We can remember before him similar maneuverings on behalf of James Baldwin and Saul Bellow and John Barth and even James Gould Cozzens. Fiction in America is haunted by gigantism. In poetry, however, the rise and fall of reputations respond to different forces. Mere size in poetry is not necessary evidence of majority, though few know what is.

Perhaps fortunately, there are few objective standards. W. H. Auden, with a characteristic mixture of pedagogy and insight, has set down some suggestive rules in his *19th Century British Minor Poets:*

> One cannot say that a major poet writes better poems than a minor; on the contrary the chances are that, in the course of his lifetime, the major poet will write more bad poems than the minor.....To qualify as major, a poet, it seems to me, must satisfy about three and a half of the following five conditions.
>
> 1. He must write a lot.
> 2. His poems must show a wide range in subject matter and treatment.
> 3. He must exhibit an unmistakable originality of vision and style.
> 4. He must be a master of verse technique.
> 5. In the case of all poets we distinguish between their juvenilia and their mature work, but [the major poet's] process of maturing continues until he dies.

Though Mr. Auden himself clearly satisfies at least four of these conditions, he is not a native American, and, no doubt for that reason, he omits one criterion that most born American poets would probably put at the top of their lists in one form or another: the major poet tries harder, is more ambitious, more "serious," has a sense of hugeness and grandeur. Mr. Auden feels no urge to dominate a continent, though others may.

Two of the American poets who could be thought in the running to pass Mr. Auden's tests are Robert Lowell and James Dickey. In most respects they are as different as American poets can be. Lowell is a son of New England; Dickey, of the South. Lowell comes from and makes much of one of America's great aristocratic families; Dickey writes as a Populist without politics. Lowell looks constantly to the civilized past—to Rome (both pagan Rome and Christian Rome), to the puritan ethic and the puritan neurosis, to the city (both in Europe and in America), to the dramatic aspects of poetry, to the sound of voices, to the tradition of Coleridge and Matthew Arnold and T. S. Eliot. Dickey, no less learned than Lowell, carries the literary past more lightly, but his poems explore our overgrown forest of archetypal scenes and situations; they deal with animals and hunting, with war and wounds, with drowning and flying; with domestic life rather than family history; with pantheism rather than Catholicism; with death and transfiguration rather than funerals; with transformations of shapes and states of being rather than with the damage wrought by time and society. In form, Lowell leans toward the elegy, the dramatic monologue, the verse play; Dickey toward the dithyramb, the narrative, the sermon. Lowell looks to the Atlantic Ocean and across it, Dickey to the great American wilderness and within the continent.

Robert Lowell has been publishing work of the first quality for over twenty years, and he has received ample recognition almost from the start. A privately printed volume, *Land of Unlikeness* (1944), was soon followed by *Lord Weary's Castle* (1946), which, incorporating the earlier volume, was immediately rewarded with a Pulitzer Prize. Lowell was barely thirty. *Lord Weary's Castle* was notable not only for the force and intensity of the poems it contained but for the complexity and variety with which it echoed the literary and cultural assumptions of the day. These years just after World War II were the heyday of American Studies in the universities, of a self-conscious literary nationalism. *Lord Weary's Castle*, despite its Scottish title, was full of allusions to the principal figures and settings of the American literary tradition: Jonathan Edwards, Hawthorne, Melville (the Melville of *Moby Dick* and *Billy*

Budd), Salem, New Bedford, Nantucket, Boston, and grave-yards, graveyards, graveyards. The New England of this book and of the next, *The Mills of the Kavanaughs*, was a bleak helpless landscape filling up with the dead and memories of the dead. The puritan ethic and its failures were violently contrasted with the presence everywhere in the poems of Roman Catholic ritual, for in those days Lowell had been received into the Catholic faith and had not yet left it.

Heaven and earth showed themselves in the repeatedly opposed symbols of the rainbow and the whale, those lightest and heaviest of things: "Atlantic, you are fouled with the blue sailors,/Sea-monsters, upward angel, downward fish." The violence and terror that have always lain at the heart of Lowell's poetry were there in plenty:

> The bones cry for the blood of the white whale,
> The fat flukes arch and whack about its ears,
> The death-lance churns into the sanctuary, tears
> The gun-blade swingle, heaving like a flail,
> And hacks the coiling life out. . . .

In *Lord Weary's Castle* and *The Mills of the Kavanaughs* (1951), the theme was *memento mori*, and it was as much a social and prophetic indictment hurled at decaying New England as it was an echo of the late-medieval, plague-haunted absorption with the facts of death and decay. Corruption lay at the heart of the New England achievement in the capture of slaves, the slaughter of whales, the imposition of theocracy, and the death of ancestors. The early poems of Lowell circled obsessively around the presence of original sin but held out no hope for the bestowal of grace.

The Mills of the Kavanaughs is the most richly melodic, the most hieratic, the most New-England-haunted of all Lowell's work. The stylistic influence of John Crowe Ransom is more evident in this book than in any before or since. It is today the least accessible and the least notorious of Lowell's books, and it contained (as had *Lord Weary*) a few "imitations," poems in which Lowell used a model from a foreign language to write a poem of his own which resembled, and in certain respects translated, the original. He has made dramatic versions of Racine's *Phèdre*, of stories by Hawthorne and Melville, of Aeschylus' *Prometheus Bound;* and he has published a whole volume of imitations of lyrics and satirical poems from numerous languages which he cannot himself read.

For some years after the appearance of *The Mills of the Kavanaughs* Lowell appeared to be floundering in search of a new poetic style, having abandoned the rich textures that he had embroidered in his first two books:

> . . . you trip and lance
> Your finger at a crab. It strikes. You rub
> It inch-meal to a bilge of shell. You dance
> Child-crazy over tub and gunnel, grasping
> Your pitchfork like a trident, poised to stab
> The greasy eel-grass clasping and unclasping
> The jellied iridescence of the crab.

This is preternatural writing, of the kind that the sea and its contents often seem to arouse in Lowell: teeming, aggressive, chaotic, frenzied, gulping at violence for the taste of it.

Lowell's next phase was heavily, absorbedly, reminiscent. During the fifties he wrote poems about history, elegies to his friends, evocations of his family. In the last section of *Life Studies* (1959) he suddenly abandoned all rhetoric, all dogma, all evasion, all displacement of violence, and spoke as himself, naked, in "Man and Wife":

> Tamed by *Miltown,* we lie on Mother's bed;
> the rising sun in war paint dyes us red;
> in broad daylight her gilded bed-posts shine. . . .
> All night I've held your hand,
> as if you had
> a fourth time faced the kingdom of the mad—
> its hackneyed speech, its homicidal eye—

Or in "Skunk Hour":

> One dark night,
> My Tudor Ford climbed the hill's skull;
> I watched for love-cars. Lights turned down,
> they lay together, hull to hull,
> where the graveyard shelves on the town. . . .
> My mind's not right. . . .
>
> I myself am hell;
> nobody's here—

These poems were shocking in their confessional directness, and they struck their first readers with terrific impact. As one of its reviewers, I must confess that my admiration for this book was at first outweighed by my discomfort. Viewed in the perspective of Lowell's total work, *Life Studies* now seems to me his highest achievement.

The synthesis of *Life Studies* was consolidated in *For the Union Dead* (1964), which contains some masterful pieces but also much that is trivial — fleeting and unresolved recollections of the past, friendships, love. The patrician begins to reassert himself. There is renewed talk of law, of the decadence of the present day. The magnificent title poem contains all these elements. The Boston monument to Robert Gould Shaw and his Civil War Negro troops has a Latin motto that says "They gave up everything to save the state." But the poet calls on childhood memories of the South Boston Aquarium, when a teacher gave his class "an unhealthy, eager, little lecture on the sewage-consumption of the conger eel." The contrast is drawn once again between New England's tradition ("On a thousand small town New England greens, / the old white churches hold their air / of sparse, sincere rebellion"), its illusions (". . . Hiroshima boiling / over a Mosler Safe, the 'Rock of Ages' / that survived the blast"), and its actuality:

> The Aquarium is gone. Everywhere,
> giant finned cars nose forward like fish;

> a savage servility
> slides by on grease.

This book, it seemed, was Lowell's farewell to Boston. Once more it looked as though his autobiographical effort had left him beached. He was, once more, turning to a more generalized past and prophesying on the American Experience; but there is more of the whale than the rainbow in his new work. In *Near the Ocean* (1967) he is gasping for air. Even in appearance it differs from his earlier books: it is bulkier, more expensive, decorated with uninspired drawings by the Australian artist Sidney Nolan, padded out to look grand. And it has returned to some of the themes of *Lord Weary's Castle* ("... one more line / unravelling from the dark design / spun by God and Cotton Mather"). The book contains only seven new original poems, none very long; the balance, 71 out of its 128 pages, are imitations, mainly from the Roman. Lowell has written better.

The new poems reveal more clearly than his past work the tug-of-war between the impulse to personal poetry on the one hand, and the Imperial Style on the other. Alas, the Emperor has won out, the Napoleon who has so often served as a character in Lowell's poems.

The opening poem in *Near the Ocean*, "Waking Early Sunday Morning," was first printed in the *New York Review of Books* in August, 1965. In its original version it was stupendous. For almost the first time in his career, Lowell had in one poem brought the squalor and disappointment of personal life into collision with the horrendous impersonal forces in the world. For some reason, however, he thought better of this poem before including it in *Near the Ocean*, and in its 1967 version numerous lines have been deleted and weak substitutions have been made. The deleted lines are in italics:

> Oh to break loose like the chinook
> salmon jumping and falling back,

nosing up to the impossible
stone and bone-crushing waterfall. . . .

Time to grub up and junk the year's
output, a dead wood of dry verse:
dim confession, coy revelation,
liftings, listless self-imitation,
whole days when I could hardly speak,
came pluming home unshaven, weak
and willing to read anyone
things done before and better done. . . .

More significantly, perhaps, compare these two versions
of the ninth stanza. Is the later version in any real respect an
improvement on the earlier?

1965

Empty, irresolute, ashamed,
when the sacred texts are named,
I lie here on my bed apart,
and when I look into my heart,
I discover none of the great
subjects: death, friendship, love and hate—
only old china doorknobs, sad,
slight useless things to calm the mad.

1967

When will we see Him face to face?
Each day, He shines through darker glass.
In this small town where everything
is known, I see His vanishing
emblems, His white spire and flag-
pole sticking out above the fog,
like old white china doorknobs, sad,
slight, useless things to calm the mad.

Is not the second version the more elevated but the less
poetic? Has not the author withdrawn himself and sent an
understudy? Is not the new voice that of the custodian of
culture rather than the poet? The 1965 version oscillates with
increasing intensity between the public and the private

dilemma, back and forth with perfect emotional rhythm, until the poem's great humming conclusion:

> peace to our children when they fall
> in small war on the heels of small
> war—until the end of time
> to police the earth, a ghost
> orbiting forever lost
> in our monotonous sublime.

The 1965 version stretches the imagination taut between the private and the public agony until we can hardly bear it; the 1967 version, its stanzas' order chopped and changed, becomes a sermon on the inefficacy of religion to calm the savagery of our time.

Would that one knew why this poem, and the others in *Near the Ocean*, should have been made so grim, cold, dutiful. As in his earlier work, Lowell locates the destructive element in the sea, in marine images of horror and fascination. Now, however, the terrible attraction of the swallowing sea becomes aligned with his Old Roman comparison between the Golden Age and the present corruption—as though, standing near the ocean, he were horribly compelled to plunge into New England waters and strike out hopelessly for the shores of the Old World. The personal style has faded away, and the poetry of *imperium* has won its victory over the Virgin, and there is little left but resignation:

> Sleep, sleep. The ocean, grinding stones,
> can only speak the present tense;
> nothing will age, nothing will last,
> or take corruption from the past.

James Dickey began publishing poetry in 1957; and in an explosive ten years his work has developed in remarkable ways technically and imaginatively, yet all his poetry has dealt with the same central concern. The world is not for him a classical structure of society based on a City governed by law, with a terrible ocean nibbling at its edges. For Dickey the world has depth and dimensions that can be explored only by a sensibility that penetrates deeper and deeper beneath the guises of reality in the hope of finding a unity at the center. His poetry is, in the words of his poem "Buckdancer's Choice," "the thousand variations of one song." Unlike Lowell, whose work had matured in technique before he was thirty, Dickey, starting from scratch at thirty-four, brought a fully inhabited imagination to his work, but he had to find his own technique, a rhetoric that would enable his ideas and sensations to move freely in verse. It took him almost ten years to reach his full powers.

How was he to express his mystical intentions in concrete images? At the outset his poems sought elemental strength similar to the simple, gentle, poignant language of Edwin Muir. Lines like these, opening "The Heaven of Animals,"

> Here they are. The soft eyes open.
> If they have lived in a wood
> It is a wood.
> If they have lived on plains
> It is grass rolling
> Under their feet forever . . .

bear a blood relation to the mysterious magnificence of Muir's "The Animals":

> They do not live in the world,
> Are not in time and space.
> From birth to death hurled
> No word do they have, not one
> To plant a foot upon,
> Were never in any place.

The similarity is more than stylistic. The older Scottish poet concerned himself with the same range of urgencies as Dickey: the "archaic companionship" of man and nature; the appearances of God in the world; the spirits of animals, trees, and water; the symbols of dream; the mysteries of flying and drowning in elements other than earth. Stylistically, Dickey's rhythms imitated Muir's in being unpretentious, conventional, deliberately unruffled; but there were more turbulent currents to trouble Dickey's underground river than Muir's still waters.

Dickey's work is a search, in a sense, for heaven on earth. He seeks order and resonance in the inchoate; ransacks through obsession, through trial and error, changes of costume and skin, through transformation of personality and the accidents of experience, to discover some sort of relation between the human and animal worlds, a bridge between the flesh and the spirit, and, more than these a link between the living and the dead. One source of this concern, frequently reiterated in *Into the Stone* (1960) and *Drowning With Others* (1962), emerges in reference to his dead brother:

> I look in myself for the being
> I was in a life before life. . . .
>
> I cannot remember my brother;
> Before I was born he went from me
> Ablaze with the meaning of typhoid.

This brother is radiant with life in the poet's dreams and in his fantasies of companionship and resurrection. He is an alter ego which borrows the poet's body and connects the poet with the world outside.

But he is hardly the only medium. Dickey's atavistic vision is like an echo, taking on shapes that shift into one another imperceptibly, unpredictably, mystically, as in "Inside the River":

> Break this. Step down.
> Follow your right
> Foot nakedly in
> To another body.
> Put on the river
> Like a floating coat,
> A garment of motion,
> Tremendous, immortal. . . .
>
> Live like the dead
> In their flying feeling.

Drowning and hunting are frequent images in the early poems. To drown is to become one with water, one with the dead. To drown in nature is to die on behalf of it, to enrich nature by losing yourself. Those who live are already the dying; only the dead therefore are spared the threat of extinction.

In his first two books Dickey had already established his poetic identity as a man restless within the confines of himself who must always be putting on other shapes (armor, helmets, hides, feathers, water) so as never to be only a single self, so as to become others, to rescue others ("The Lifeguard" is a particularly interesting poem on this theme). He remarks with amazement: "Someone lay with his body shaken / Free of the self. . . ." The ultimate way of becoming more than the self is to die. Dying unites us with others, with the animals, with the animal in ourselves; and the only way to understand the secret of death is to penetrate, to thrust, to cleave beyond the surfaces of nature to the ultimate kinship.

However, his technique was still at some distance behind his aspirations. He was handicapped as a poet by having come to his craft late, already knowing what he wanted to say, but not how to say it. Most of the poems in the first two books, as also in *Helmets* (1964), leave the reader with the feeling that the poem has begun at the wrong place, or ended too late, after the reader's attention has already been used up.

Yet there are vibrant exceptions, like "Fence Wire," "Cherrylog Road," "The Scarred Girl," and "Drinking from a Helmet." In the last, several of Dickey's obsessive themes join forces: during World War II the poet is in a line of soldiers waiting for water. He sees his face reflected in the water in a dead man's helmet: "I kept trembling forward through something / Just born of me." To see himself in another's helmet brings back once again Dickey's sense of substituting for his dead brother: "I knew / That I inherited one of the dead." The poem leads the poet backward in time, "into the wood / Until we were lost." Dickey had yet to discover a

technique that would liberate him from his natural limitations—or else one that would take advantage of them. This
poem, the last in *Helmets*, may have been a turning point. It
brought him face to face with the memory of war, with the
painfulness of the past remembered, and it embodied his
theme in a narrative setting. He could no longer confine
himself to sequences of images clustered around a central
statement which was often weaker and less pungent than the
images themselves, and sometimes even banal. He had to find
a method which would enable him to move backward and
forward in time as well as in space, and he had to escape from
the tyranny of the dactylic drone.

With *Buckdancer's Choice* (1965) Dickey began to break
free, and also to establish a reputation. He now opened up
and exploited the possibilities of narrative — poetic narrative,
not mere prose narrative in verse. Moreover, his liberation
seemed to be accompanied by a liberation of violence, as
though personal memories and poetic themes alike had long
been suppressed. Now he began recovering for poetry his war
experiences. Was it the memory of war, opened up almost
twenty years afterward, that suggested new rhythms to him?
Or was it the fighter pilot's memory of flying? Both themes,
hereafter in his work, made their presence more keenly felt
than before. More urgent, too, is the reality of the past side
by side with the present. A new metric, a new emphasis on
narrative, the exploration of new themes and the extension
of old ones, a freer use of the dimension of time—these four
elements distinguish Dickey's maturity from his early work.
In his themes of communion with the dead and the kinship
of nature, he had established the possibility of a new voice in
American poetry as clear as that of Theodore Roethke; but
to attain it, he would have to win through to the clarity of
Roethke's vision and to the resonance of Roethke's music.

The three major poems in *Buckdancer's Choice* are "The
Firebombing," "The Fiend," and "Slave Quarters." All three
have taken on narrative progression, and all three skip in

great leaps backward and forward in time and space. A fourth
narrative, "The Shark's Parlor," is a carnival of violence
which falls short of success because the poet declines into his
old habit of summing up at the end, in a moral which might
have suited a poem of images but which is out of place in a
poem of narration. "The Firebombing" explores the relation
between the corpulent householder of 1965 and the napalm-
scattering pilot on a run over Japan of twenty years earlier:
"when those on earth / Die, there is not even sound. . . ."

> It is this detachment,
> The honored aesthetic evil,
> The greatest sense of power in one's life,
> That must be shed in bars, or by whatever
> Means, by starvation
> Visions in well-stocked pantries . . .
> > I swing
> Over directly over the heart
> The *heart* of the fire. . . .

"The Fiend" is a dazzling performance in its characterization
of a middle-aged Peeping Tom and his transcendent relationship with the women he peers at from trees and bushes at
night. This poem is the first of more to follow that explore
the realms of sexual aberrance:

> > It will take years
> But at last he will shed his leaves burn his roots give up
> Invisibility will step out will make himself known to the one
> He cannot see loosen her blouse take off luxuriously with lips
> Compressed against her mouth-stain her dress her stockings
> Her magic underwear.

In these poems the mature technique makes itself manifest:
long lines with stresses far apart, emphatic pauses punctuated
by typographical spaces, frequent repetition of words and
rhythms, looping syntax. Sometimes the old dactylic cadence
appears, especially in short poems, but it is much altered in
the direction of subtlety.

The full power of Dickey's poetry becomes apparent in
the new part of his new book, *Poems 1957-1967* (Wesleyan

University Press). The breakthrough goes even beyond what might have been expected.

> I have had my time   dressed up as something else,
> Have thrown time off my track by my disguise.

The rhythms are now remarkable indeed, and flexible as acrobats:

> She was a living-in-the-city
> Country girl   who on her glazed porch broke off
> An icicle, and bit through its blank bone: brought me
> Into another life   in the shining-skinned clapboard house
> Surrounded by a world where creatures could not stand,
> Where people broke hip after hip.

Dickey's oldest theme, that of man's reincarnation as angel, returns in strange and novel form:

> I always had
> These wings   buried deep in my back:
> There is a wing-growing motion
> Half-alive in every creature.

It emerges again in "Falling," a very long but not really successful poem about a stewardess who falls from an airliner and strips as she falls. In "The Sheep-Child" he investigates a theme as old as the Minotaur, sexual relations between man and beast, in terrifying eloquence:

> I saw for a blazing moment
> The great grassy world from both sides,
> Man and beast in the round of their need. . . .

In "Sun," "Power and Light," "Adultery" (". . . me with my grim techniques. Or you who have sealed your womb / With a ring of convulsive rubber"), he deals with domestic relations and the love-hate between man and woman. In "Encounter in the Cage Country" he returns once again to the animals, but with a wolfish intensity that is new:

>   the crowd
> Quailed from me   I was inside and out
> Of myself   and something was given a life-

Mission to say to me hungrily over

And over and over   your moves are exactly right
For a few things in this world: we know you
When you come, Green Eyes, Green Eyes.

All of Dickey's development, and all of his thematic complexity, are wrapped up in one long poem which opens *Poems 1957-1967.* "May Day Sermon to the Women of Gilmer County, Georgia, by a Woman Preacher Leaving the Baptist Church" contains everything that Dickey, at this stage, can put into a poem. The new metric and syntax are there; the obsessive theme of death and renewal and repetition and eternity; the transformations of the earth-bound, the archetypes of country life. It strains toward universality. Only time will tell whether it retains it; but this poem contains in one place everything James Dickey has been developing toward.

If American poetry needs a champion for the new generation, Dickey's power and ambition may supply the need. His archetypal concerns are universal to all languages and will no doubt carry over into translation; his sense of urgency is overwhelming; his volume, his range, his style, his technique, his process of maturing—all might supply W. H. Auden's five categories (and so might the number of bad poems he has written!). There is no need for pessimism, yet there may continue to be a danger of overblowing. Such writing as Dickey's requires a vast fire to keep the caldron boiling. If he were to encounter a slight recession of energy, such as that which seems lately to have overtaken Robert Lowell, Dickey's value as a poet might easily enter into a decline just at the moment when his reputation, like Lowell's today, has reached its apogee.

Chapter III

THE WAY OF EXCHANGE IN JAMES DICKEY'S POETRY
by H. L. Weatherby

At least one way of judging the quality of a poet's work is to decide how close he comes to realizing what he set out to do. In the case of James Dickey the intention is fairly clear—to find some light which is not "too feeble to show/my world as I knew it must be." The complexity arises when we try to show how, and how well, he achieves this.

The passage I have just quoted is from "The Owl King," which appears in the 1958 volume, *Drowning with Others*. It is neither so good a poem nor so good a collection as the subsequent ones, *Helmets* (1962) and *Buckdancer's Choice* (1964), which are our present concern; but in several of these earlier poems we find Dickey developing the images through which in the later poetry he is to go about seeing his world. A poem from the earlier collection which will serve our purposes very well is "A Dog Sleeping on my Feet." Here the

The phrase "the way of exchange" belongs originally to Charles Williams. However, my use of it involved no conscious reference to Williams's work, and it is debatable whether Williams's understanding of "exchange" would throw any light on James Dickey's poetry.

From *The Sewanee Review, LXXIV*, 3 (Summer, 1966), © 1966 by The University of the South. Reprinted by permission of the author and the publisher.

situation is a simple one, but one which provides a vehicle for most of Dickey's recurrent themes. A fox hound is asleep on a man's leg, and the man is a poet, writing while the hound sleeps and writing about what is being transmitted from the dog's life into his own. "For now, with my feet beneath him/dying like embers,/the poem is beginning to move/up through my pine-prickling legs/out of the night wood,/taking hold of the pen by my fingers."

The result of this transmission is, we imply, the sort of poem Dickey wants to write, one in which the light is sufficiently strong to see the world as it *really* is. Moreover the poem makes it clear how the poet goes about getting this light, and, in seeing how, we get to the heart of all Dickey's poetry, early and late. The light seems to come from some rather mysterious process of exchange between a man and his opposites. In this poem and a great many others the opposition and exchange is between men and animals, but, as we shall see later, it may also occur between men who are opposed to each other by nationality, between the living and the dead, between men and trees, and even between men and wrecked machinery. However, in each of these instances, the same thing happens which occurs here between a man and a dog. Therefore this poem can be used as a key to what I would regard as the central pattern in all Dickey's poetry. By entering into the dog the poet participates in the dog's experience of the chase:

> Before me the fox floats lightly,
> On fire with his holy scent.
> All, all are running.
> Marvelous is the pursuit,
> Like a dazzle of nails through the ankles,
>
> Like a twisting shout through the trees
> Sent after the flying fox
> Through the holes of logs, over streams
> Stock-still with the pressure of moonlight.
> My killed legs,
> My legs of a dead thing, follow,

> Quick as pins, through the forest,
> And all rushes on into the dark
> And ends on the brightness of paper.

Then, when the dog gets up, the poet's hand "shall falter, and fail/back into the human tongue." Through the dog he has been able to see the hunt as he "knew it must be"—the holiness of the scent, the marvellous nature of the pursuit. In other words, the exchange has produced an immediacy of perception which the poet without the dog could never have achieved.

However, as one can see immediately, there is more to the exchange than that. This experience is by no means a simple matter of a man's projecting himself into the beast for the purpose of understanding. The poem which is the product of the exchange presents not simply a dog's perception but a composite vision which is both human and animal at once. In other words the exchange is literally that—an entrance not only of man into dog, but also of dog into man. Dickey is careful never to let this fact out of our sight; the dog's immediate participation in violent scent and movement is fixed and stilled by his participation in the man's intellect. Notice, for instance, that the streams are "stock-still with the pressure of moonlight". In fact all the movement of the poem is motionless; the rushing in the dark ends in absolute, while stillness "on the brightness of paper." Moreover, the dog's running legs are the poet's "killed legs," asleep where the dog is sleeping on them; and this joint participation in sleep is itself important. For the exchange to become possible the opposites, the man and the dog, must die to each other. The dog must give up his immediate perception to the man and the man must give up his power of reflection, his power to fix and see, to the dog, so that in the giving and taking, the mutual surrender, a new and otherwise impossible point of view can be created.

What this new point of view sees is by no means new; in fact the paradox of motionless motion, the still point of the turning world, the perfect union of man and his opposites, the *me* and the *not me*, is what poetry always tries to express. Even Dickey's images, in this poem at least, are not very original. The still stream reminds one of Wordworth's stationary blasts of waterfalls in Simplon Pass; the chase motionless on white is reminiscent of Keat's urn; and the terms in which Dickey presents the paradoxical relationship between animal life and rational death suggest Yeat's Byzantium poems. But the effort to resolve these paradoxes through the process of exchange which we have just examined may very well be unique with Dickey. If that is true it may be safe to say that he has achieved a new way of doing what all poets do or try to do in one way or another, for Simplon Pass, the urn, and Byzantium are all efforts to throw a light on the world which will show it as the poet knows it must be.

I like the owl's metaphor of a light in which to see what *really* is (and it is significant that the owl courts the child in order to see). There are certain days, usually in April and May, when the quality of light is different from what it is at any other time, and in this new quality you can see details of leaves, of houses, and of the contours of land which you have never noticed before. As a result you feel that you have discovered the way things *really* are, as you always knew they must be—what a magnolia tree you have looked at all your life actually is. It is as if you have discovered a new landscape superimposed upon the old one, at once identical with the old one and yet at the same time more nearly coherent and intelligible and consequently more satisfying than the old one. It is this second and fuller vision of the superimposed landscape which Dickey achieves in his exchanges. Take, for instance, one more poem from *Drowning with Others*, "The Heaven of Animals." Here, through the same exchange between bestiality and reason that occurs in "A Dog Sleeping on my Feet," the animals become what we always knew they must be. In "the richest wood, the deepest field" the hunters hunt to perfection "with claws and teeth grown perfect,/ more deadly than they can believe." And their prey also fulfill themselves, knowing "this as their life,/their reward: to walk/under such trees in full knowledge/of what is in glory above them,/and to feel no fear,/but acceptance, compliance." That is, we infer, what a forest really is like, but it can only be seen as that—in fact it can only become that—in Byzantium, or at the "still point," or at the point of exchange, of composite vision, in mutual surrender between man and the animals.

The poems in *Helmets* (1962) touch the exchange again and again. Take, for instance, "Approaching Prayer". To "fall to my knees/and produce a word I can't say" the poet must have all his reason "slain." It is again the process of death by which the speaker in the earlier poem enters the dog and allows the dog to enter him. In "Approaching Prayer" there is actually a physical "putting on" of the beast. The son dresses in his father's old hunting sweater, straps the spurs of gamecocks on his heels, and places on his head the head of the boar he himself has shot in his "own best and stillest moment." Now, in the exchange, that still moment becomes a moment of "murderous stillness" in which the poet is able to use the "images of earth/almightily," in order "for something important to be." He is able to see himself shooting the boar through the eyes of the boar who is being shot, and in so doing the killer and the killed change places, are united, and are enabled by the union to play their respective parts perfectly. Both are able to participate in the glory of killing and in the acceptance, compliance, of the killed. This is the heaven of both hunters and animals.

Or take other instances:

In "Springer Mountain" the hunter strips himself; and in the loss of his four sweaters and dungarees "the world catches fire" from his naked flesh, and he "puts an unbearable light/into breath skinned alive of its garments." Naked like the buck and running with him he is able to think

"like a beast loving/with the whole god bone of his horns."
By entering into the deer he makes it possible for deer to
become what they really are in relationship to men. In the
superimposed landscape established by the exchange deer
stamp and dream of men

> Who will kneel with them naked to break
> The ice from streams with their faces
> And drink from the lifespring of beasts.

And notice that again the waters from which they are to
drink together "stand petrified in a creek bed/yet melt and
flow from the hills/at the touch of an animal visage."

In "Chenille," the poems are the bedspreads—not those
products of mass manufacture which "hum like looms all
night/into your pores" but those made by a "middle-aged
man's grandmother" in the "summer green light" of a
scuppernong arbor. These embody the composite vision of
the exchange; each spread becomes a "heaven of animals"—

> Deer, rabbits and birds,
> Red whales and unicorns,
> Winged elephants, crowned ants:
> Beasts that cannot be thought of
>   By the wholly sane
> Rise in the rough, blurred
> Flowers of fuzzy cloth
> In only their timeless outlines
> Like the beasts of Heaven:
> Those sketched out badly, divinely
> By stars not wholly sane.

The grandmother like the poet has seen what animals *really*
are. Moreover, we infer that the rest of us, who are too
"wholly sane" to exchange our nature with a dog or a horse,
will miss the summer peace of a scuppernong arbor or the
winter peace of sleep with our arms around the neck of a
unicorn. We shall know instead only the constant hum of
factories.

As I have said, however, the exchange need not necessarily be with animals, and in some of Dickey's best poems it is not. In "Cherrylog Road" the man exchanges his life not only with beetles and snakes but also with a woman and even with a junkyard. On account of the sexual exchange between the boy and the girl, snakes and beetles in the wreckage, dying of boredom, come to life again; and of course the act of copulation in which the human beings participate is itself something exchanged with the beasts. However, it is not just the animals in the wreckage but the wreckage itself that participates in man, and he in it. In the act of love the couple is "convoyed at terrific speed/by the stalled, dreaming traffic around us"; the motorcycle becomes "the soul of the junkyard/restored, a bicycle fleshed/with power"; and, on the other side of the exchange, the man, having taken the junkyard into himself, is "wild to be wreckage forever."

"The Driver" is reminiscent of "Cherrylog Road" except that in this underwater junkyard of war machinery we have, instead of animals dying of boredom, dead human beings. Moreover, the exchange which the poet attempts is not with the wreckage but with the dead themselves. The swimmer is "haunted," and that is "to sink out of sight, and to lose/the power of speech in the presence/of the dead." In short, to be haunted is to take upon oneself the condition of the dead, to be possessed by the dead, and that is what the swimmer almost does. He attempts to enter the dead in the same way that he enters the dog, the boar, the deer, the woman, or the wreckage. Again we see Dickey attempting to establish a composite vision, but there are two interesting variations here. In the first place, at the last possible moment, the swimmer refuses the exchange; he leaps "for the sky/very nearly too late, where another/leapt and could not break into/his breath." Moreover, the dead are also incapable of the exchange; unlike the buck they do not enter into the experience of the poet. They have failed to "break into/his breath, where it lay, in battle/as in peace, available, secret,/dazzling and huge, filled with sunlight,/for thousands of miles on the water." The boundary between water and air prevents the exchange between the dead and the living; the swimmer can only toy with the possibility.

"The Driver" anticipates a number of poems in Dickey's latest volume in which the exchange does fail. However, in "Drinking from a Helmet," with which *Helmets* closes, the exchange between living and dead is accomplished. A reflection in the water in a dead man's helmet gives the boy back his own face, "in its [the dead's] absence holding/my sealed, sunny image from harm" in the middle of battle. Then, when he puts on the helmet, the dead man's past enters his own experience; so the dead man's image is likewise preserved and with it his family and his past which are, of course, his life—California, the redwoods, a bicycle, and "his blond brother." These are the details of the superimposed landscape; the redwoods and the shelled palm stumps meet in the "rings of a bodiless tree," formed in the water in the helmet.

Buckdancer's Choice contains the best poetry in the three collections. One reason for the improvement is simply Dickey's growing ability to make language do what it is supposed to do. However, in addition to this there is also in this later poetry a new sense of the consequences of the exchange. The dog wakes up and so do the man's legs; at that point the poet returns to human speech. The hunter in "Springer Mountain" gets back finally into his clothes. But to take the exchange seriously is to risk staying under, and the best poems in *Buckdancer's Choice* show an awareness of this risk.

Among the finest of these is "Pursuit from Under," in which the poet, through "the journal of Arctic explorers," is able to experience, in August on his father's farm, "the cold of a personal ice age," the terror of the killer whale who follows always "under the frozen pane,/turning as you do, zigzagging," until he finally shatters through and confronts both the explorers and the poet in their exchange of understanding with "an image/of how the downed dead pursue us." The explorers have had the vision of the snow, the poet the vision of the family field, but in the new landscape of the exchange the explorers know

> That not only in the snow
> But in the family field
>
> The small shadow moves,
> And under bare feet in the summer:
> That somewhere turf will heave,
> And the outraged breath of the dead,
> So long held, will form
>
> Unbreathably around the living.

And the poet knows that instead of walking barefoot "so that nothing on earth can have changed/on the ground where I was raised" he will now have to "pitch a tent in the pasture, and starve."

Another sign that Dickey is aware of the danger is the presence in this last volume of a number of poems in which, as in "The Driver," the cost of the exchange makes it impossible. "The Firebombing" is one of these. The poet has dropped napalm on a Japanese village from cold blue heights of "aesthetic contemplation," and isolated in those heights he finds that he cannot enter "the *heart* of the fire." Even at the end of twenty years in his own suburban residence he is still unable "to get down there or see/what really happened." The reason?—that he has never been able to take upon himself the suffering of the Japanese as he could take upon himself the dreams of a dog or the head of a boar. He cannot imagine at his own "unfired door" a person burning, "with its ears crackling off/like powdery leaves" or "with children of ashes." In fact he can imagine nothing at his door that he hasn't lived with twenty years, and in that fact alone we see the failure of the exchange which is always between opposites—dead men and live men, the suffering and the secure.

"The Shark's Parlor" is another poem about the failure,

but this time a comic one. The bloodstain in "our vacation paradise" is somewhat like the personal ice age in the family field, but this time instead of pitching a tent and starving the poet is still using the place for vacations. And that is what you do, I suppose; when you realize that you have not been man enough to stay under or to look the killer whale or the "drowned dead" in the eye, you laugh a little ruefully and cherish the bloodstain you acquired trying.

"The Fiend," if I understand it correctly, is a much more serious poem about the same failure. The voyeur never finally exchanges his nature with the trees from which he peeps. As a consequence he ends in sordid cheapness "like a door-to-door salesman/the godlike movement of trees stiffening with him the light/of a hundred favored windows gone wrong somewhere in his glasses/where his knocked-off panama hat was in his painfully vanishing hair." To exchange life with death is serious enough, but to take upon yourself the "godlike movement" of nature is more serious still. Moreover, if it doesn't work, the failure can in fact produce a fiend. If a man tries to take the natural into himself without in turn giving himself to it, he has not redeemed nature by creating an animal heaven or, in this case, a heaven of trees, but he has brutalized himself instead. There is simply taking, no exchange, which is, interestingly enough, the nature of voyeurism.

I suggested at the outset that at least one way to measure a poet is by how well he has realized his intentions. I suppose at this point it will be perfectly obvious that I think James Dickey is a very fine poet who has attempted to see his world in a remarkable way and has had considerable success in doing so. However, I hold one reservation which seems to me worth stating. The way of exchange is as dangerous a thing aesthetically as it is spiritually, and whereas Dickey's later poems show that he is fully aware of the spiritual danger, I am by no means sure that he has guarded himself sufficiently against the aesthetic. There is always something a little bit staged, exotic, preposterous, and consequently affected about Dickey's situations. All of them lend themselves to parody except those like "The Shark's Parlor" which parody themselves, and if a reader is tempted to giggle when he shouldn't it always means that the poet has fallen short of complete success. I am deeply moved by a poem like "Springer Mountain," but I cannot help being slightly amused at the same time by the softening, middle-aged man's running naked with the buck. In the same way there is something mildly preposterous about putting on cock's spurs and a boar's head in order to pray. As the language in the later poetry grows stronger there is less and less opportunity for the ludicrous, but even here there is sometimes a hint of it—something a little bit silly about pitching a tent in the field and starving with cattle all around.

The reason for this weakness in the poetry is that the kind of vision which Dickey attempts, and in part achieves, requires a great deal of the reader's imagination. By staring intently in a certain light you may eventually see your world as you know it must be, but you may also break under the strain of the staring. According to Christian doctrine, when Nature is redeemed through our Lord's exchange with the dead, men and sharks, lions and lambs, Japanese and Americans, the hunters and the hunted, will all lie down together in a new landscape under a light strong enough and constant enough to show us our world as we have all known always that it must be—and without any strain of staring. Short of that, poetry can, as we know, give us some anticipation of those "other worlds and other seas," but it has been only the very greatest poets—Dante, Spenser, Shakespeare, and possibly Yeats—who have managed it with complete success. Obviously any effort toward this vision that does not take into consideration the aesthetic equivalent of the passion and death is going to wind up sounding fixed and dishonest. For the poet as poet there can be no last-minute leap to the surface for air, no hesitation to undergo his sea change or enter into the heart of the fire. Short of that sacrifice a poetry which attempts such a vision will prove in the last analysis to be affected. That is why most great poetry is tragic, dealing only with the impossibility of the vision.

In his volume of criticism *The Suspect in Poetry*, which was published in 1964 but which contains reviews of contemporary poets published over a period of several years, Dickey sets up a standard of absolute honesty by which poetry is to be judged and according to which he finds most contemporary poetry lacking. Those elements which are "suspect" in poetry are those which readers cannot "believe in as 'reality' "—a "series of unbelievable contrivances, none of which has the power of bringing forth a genuine response." Exactly how unbelievable contrivance can become is amply illustrated by Dickey's examination of people like Allen Ginsberg, Thom Gunn, or Harold Witt, and I think it is indisputable that Dickey himself is considerably above them. On the other hand he has attempted something very difficult, and it seems to me that in doing so he does risk the very contrivance that he warns against. However, I feel sure that he must be aware of the danger himself.

Chapter IV

THE WORLDLY MYSTIC
by Laurence Lieberman

The persona in James Dickey's new poems, those that appear in the final section ("Falling") of his new book,[1] is a unique human personality. He is a worldly mystic. On the one hand, a joyous expansive personality—all candor, laughter and charm—in love with his fully conscious gestures, the grace and surety of moves of his body. An outgoing man. An extrovert. On the other hand, a chosen man. A man who has been picked by some mysterious intelligent agent in the universe to act out a secret destiny:

> . . . something was given a life-
> mission to say to me hungrily over
>
> And over and over *your moves are exactly right*
> *For a few things in this world: we know you*
> *When you come, Green Eyes, Green Eyes.*
>
> (from "Encounter in the Cage Country")

How does a man re-connect with common unchosen humanity when he has just returned from the abyss of nonhuman chosen otherness? That is the chief problem to

---

1. POEMS 1957-1967, by *James Dickey*. Wesleyan.

Reprinted by permission from *The Hudson Review*, Vol. XX, No. 3 (Autumn, 1967). © 1967 by The Hudson Review, Inc.

which the final volume addresses itself. How to be a man who feels perfectly at home, and at his ease, in both worlds—the inner and outer. A man who can make of himself and his art a medium, a perfect conductor, through which the opposed worlds—both charged with intensity—can meet and connect, flow into each other. The worldly mystic. It is the vision of a man who for years has been just as committed to developing his potential for creative existence as for creative art. All discoveries and earnings, spiritual or worldly, must carry over from one universe to the other.

In the best poems of the previous volume, *Buckdancer's Choice*, the self is frustrated, paralyzed, helplessly unable to establish liberating connections with the world. The chief obstacle to self-liberation is a sense of moral guilt. In "The Firebombing," "The Fiend," and "Slave Quarters," the self is pitilessly subjected to encounters with life that induce feelings of criminality. Clearly, the writer has deliberately trapped the persona in predicaments of contemporary American life that automatically create an aura of grave moral jeopardy. In all three poems, the conflict between the worldly-mindedness of modern life and the inner life of the spirit is dramatized. Materialism, of a kind that blocks the persona in its struggle to connect with the world, is embodied in the indulgences of suburban middle-class home life of "The Firebombing"; in the business-like exterior of "The Fiend," his guise of normalcy and ordinariness; and in the catalogue of inferior occupational stereotypes, earmarked for Negroes by our society, in "Slave Quarters."

Wherever being is trapped in oneself or in others, the existential self must work, either through art or directly in life, to make life-saving connections—all those connections which create the free interchange of spirit between being and being. The word *connect* is the central one in Dickey's new poetry. His spirit must connect with the world, with "all worlds the growing encounters." In the best poems, all the connections are good. "I am a man who turns on," and when he turns on, all worlds he connects with turn on, since wherever he connects, he creates personal intimacy, injects intensity: "People are calling each other weeping with a hundred thousand/ Volts."

The one poem that perfectly reconciles the contradictions between worldliness and the inner life of the spirit is "Power and Light." The happiness of power and light heals all broken connections, "even the one/ With my wife." For the artist, the hardest connections to "turn good" may be the home connections, the ones thorny with daily ritual and sameness: "Thorns! Thorns! I am bursting/ Into the kitchen, into the sad way station/Of my home. . . ." But if the connections are good, all worlds flow into each other, the good healing, cleansing the bad. There is woe in the worldly side of marriage, but it is good in its spiritual and sexual dimensions, in the "deep sway of underground."

"Power and Light" dramatizes the secret life of a pole-climber, a technician who works for the power company. Through the disguise of the persona, Dickey explores symbolically the ideal relationship between the artist and his audience, the poet and his readers:

> . . . I feel the wires running
Like the life-force along the limed rafters and all connections
With poles with the tarred naked belly-buckled black
Trees I hook to my heels with the shrill phone calls leaping
Long distance long distances through my hands all connections

Even the one
With my wife, turn good . . . Never think I don't know my profession
Will lift me: why, all over hell the lights burn in your eyes,
People are calling each other weeping with a hundred thousand
Volts making deals pleading laughing like fate,
Far off, invulnerable or with the right word pierced

To the heart
By wires I held, shooting off their ghostly mouths,
In my gloves.

The pole-climber's spirit raises the spirits of the dead and damned from hell—marriage, too, being a kind of hell. The "ghostly mouths" of the spirits can all re-connect through the power lines—lines of the poem—and save themselves. The poet is blessed with such an access, a surplus, of lifesaving joy, he can afford to let it—the flood of power and light—overflow into the grave, into hell. He doesn't so much give life to the damned as open them up to hidden resources of life, newly accessible in themselves, by making connections. "Long distance," an eerie experience to begin with, becomes more haunting still when Dickey extends it to include connections between living and dead spirits.

Dickey proceeds in his vision to a point "far under the grass of my grave." No matter how deep he travels, even to hell, in the fuller mastery of his art he is confident "my profession/Will lift me," and in lifting him, it will lift thousands of others from hell, his readers all over the world, symbolically making long distance phone calls all night, connecting, all the connections good. He feels the same power, whether in the basement of his home, "or flung up on towers walking/Over mountains my charged hair standing on end." The spirit which pervades and dominates this poem, finally, can be identified as the spirit of laughter, a laughter closely akin to that of Malachi the stiltjack in Yeat's "High Talk," or the mad dancer of "A Drunken Man's Praise of Sobriety." Like these poems, "Power and Light" verges on self-parody in its hyperbolic imagery and rhetoric: "And I laugh/ Like my own fate watching over me night and day."

The comic spirit of "Power and Light" recovers the ground lost by the tragic spirit in the moral dilemmas of "The Firebombing" and "Slave Quarters." If modern man feels helpless before the massive political nightmare of his time, he finds he can retreat into "pure fires of the Self" for spiritual sustenance. This is the artist's escape and salvation. If he can't connect with the tragic people of this world's hell in daylight, by direct political action, he must reach them in the dark,/ deep sway of underground. The artist's night is the "night before Resurrection Day." He will resurrect the imagination, the spiritual life, of his Age. He performs these wonders, ironically, drunk in his suburban basement. A general in disguise. An unacknowledged legislator of the world. Regrettably, the philosophy, *if I turn on everyone turns on with me*, may offer small comfort in the political world.

If the worldly mystic spends a good portion of his day-to-day existence reconnecting with the world, at other times we find him searching for the pure moment in solitude, waiting to receive messages from the unseen beyond, and to answer the call. If he is receptive enough, he may pick up clues to learning his being from a wide range of sources: a rattlesnake, a blind old woman, a caged leopard. In all such poems, Dickey himself would seem to be the protagonist, the poem being a kind of reportage of an event from the author's life, in contrast with poems like "Power and Light" and "Falling," in which the persona and the author are completely separate, on the surface level.

"The Flash" is a weak poem, hardly more than a fragment of verse, but it gives the key to understanding the revelatory moments in the other poems in the group:

> Something far off buried deep and free
> In the country can always strike you dead
> Center of the brain. There is never anything
> It could be but you go dazzled . . .

You can't explain the flash logically, or fasten hold of it with your senses, but what is felt when "you go dazzled" is instantly recognizable, and can be distinguished, unerringly, from other events of the spirit. The flash is a spiritual fact that registers in the poet's intelligence with the same cold, tough certainty as snakebite. It is a guarantee of the inner life, but also insists on the inner life of the Other, of others "far off buried deep and free."

In "Snakebite," the encounter with the Other seems

fated. "The one chosen" finds "there is no way not/ To be me." There is no way out, or through the experience, except saving oneself:

> . . . It is the role
> I have been cast in;
>
> It calls for blood.
>
> Act it out before the wind
> Blows: unspilt blood
>
> Will kill you. Open
> The new-footed tingling. Cut.
> Cut deep, as a brother would.
> Cut to save it. Me.

One must act out the roles that are thrust upon one by the Other, inescapably, as by the rattlesnake's poison. Art must invade those moments in life when failure to perform the correct self-saving gesture is to die. Art is a strange kind of intimacy, a blood-brotherhood, between the artist and himself. The poem must be an act of blood-letting. In saving the poem, as in saving one's life from snakebite, a man must be his own brother. No one else can help.

Midway in the action, the speaker shifts from the mortal necessity of lancing the wound to a moment of comic staging. At this point in Dickey's art, it seems appropriate and convincing for the comic spirit to interrupt the most serious human act of self-preservation. The laughter of self-dramatization parallels similar moments in "Encounter in the Cage Country," in which comic relief enhances the seriousness of the exchange between man and leopard:

> . . . at one brilliant move
>
> I made as though drawing a gun from my hip-
> bone, the bite-sized children broke
> Up changing their concept of laughter,
>
> But none of this changed his eyes, or changed
> My green glasses. Alert, attentive,
> He waited for what I could give him;

> My moves   my throat   my wildest love,
> The eyes behind my eyes.

In "False Youth II," the blind grandmother's message, like the words of an oracle, is delivered with absolute certitude: "You must laugh a lot/ Or be in the sun." Her advice strikes a reader as being a deeply personal and literal truth in the author's life at the time he wrote the poem, and this hunch is borne out by the relevance her words have to many of the best poems of the new volume. A comic spirit pervades poems like "Power and Light," "Encounter in the Cage Country" and "Sun" that one had not met or foreseen in Dickey's earlier work.

Dickey presents an experience from life—in "False Youth II"—which taught him to see deeply into the shifting sands of his own personality, as he slid, imperceptibly, from youth into middle age. Youth is a "lifetime search" for the human role, or roles, which, when acted out, will serve as a spiritual passport of entry into middle age. The necessary role may take the form of a physical gesture that perfectly corresponds to deep moves of the spirit: "My face froze . . . in a smile/ That has never left me since my thirty-eighth year."

The old blind woman unknowingly assumes the role of a fortune teller. She has developed a superhumanly receptive sense of touch. Her life is contracted intensely into her hands, her fingertips having grown fantastically sensitive and alive. As she runs her fingers over his eyes and forehead, the poetic images envision a scientific and quasi-scientific composite of data linking electromagnetism, finger-printing, astronomy, genetics, and fortune-telling:

> . . . I closed my eyes as she put her fingertips lightly
> On them and saw, behind sight something in me fire
> Swirl in a great shape like a fingerprint like none other
> In the history of the earth looping holding its wild lines
> Of human force. Her forefinger then her keen nail
> Went all the way along the deep middle line of my brow

Not guessing but knowing quivering deepening
Whatever I showed by it.

The wisdom of the old woman has a primeval quality about
it. Her acutely sharpened instincts and sense of touch precede
the scientific age and surpass recorded modern science in a
revelation of human personality that draws on the learning of
many sciences, but goes beyond each in its ability to *connect*
them all: which is not to say this literally happens in life. It
happens, rather, in the images of the poem's vision.

She leads him to discover he has come to a crossroads in
his life and art. He must learn his life, as his art, and each
stage of existence—in both worlds—concludes with a search
for the blueprint to the next stage. The blueprint cannot
simply be willed into existence. It is contained as a deeply
true, hidden, map of possibility within his developing self. If
there are alternative paths latent and waiting to be journeyed
in the self at any particular spiritual crossroads (as in Frost's
poem "The Road Not Taken"), there is one best route
available at each crucial juncture. It is discoverable, and once
discovered, it has an unmistakable ring of truth: "Not
guessing but knowing quivering deepening." Though the
answer waits inside him to be released, he cannot find his
way to it by himself. He arrives in himself through a deep
conjunction with another being, in faith, "some kind of song
may have passed/ Between our closed mouths as I headed into the ice." There must be communion with the Other.
Connection.

If one of the major new themes in Dickey's fifth volume
is comic dramatization of his own personality, another is
sexual realism. In both, he parallels the later Yeats. If we
compare the vision in "The Fiend" with that in "Falling" and
"The Sheep Child," we can get an idea of how far Dickey's
art has travelled between the first major poem dealing with
the theme of sexual realism and the last. In "The Fiend," the

free-flowing form and the split line are fully exploited. This technique is well-suited to sustained psychological realism. Also, the fiend is a thoroughly convincing persona. The encounter between him and life-experience, though voyeuristic and "abnormal," is presented as final, incisive, fulfilling.

But somehow, the center of the poem's vision is too far from tragedy and believable danger: the poem lacks risk, the emotional pitch of a cosmos of love/beauty stretching to contain and transform a brutal agony of being. The sexual transcendence the persona unknowingly achieves is almost too evident, pre-given. Equipoise is not felt to be the outcome of a fierce yoking together of oppositely charged beings, as in the act of coitus between the farm boy and the mother ewe of "The Sheep Child":

> . . . It was something like love
> From another world that seized her
> From behind, and she gave, not lifting her head
> Out of dew, without ever looking, her best
> Self to that great need.

The stench of evil in "The Fiend" is smothered under the catalogues of domestic inanities. There is no trace of the searing terror of "The Sheep Child," the terror of our settled scheme of things being ripped apart. It is too easy to dismiss the fiend as a genial saint—spiritually, if not bodily, harmless. "The Sheep Child" and "Falling" threaten us with glimpses into a world of becoming that is grimly near to us, a mere hand's-reach away from those extensions of being into the beyond that we all easily attain in moments of emotional intensity. And yet, that farther reach somehow eludes us, staying just out of our ken. The secret of uncompromised being is just a spiritual stone's throw away, but we are cut off. These poems soar into that further beyond with a sense of effortlessness and inevitability.

"The Fiend" was a breakthrough into the hinterland of sexual transcendence, but what begins as a reader's sympathetic identification ends as a comfortably removed appreciation of the poem's novelties. "The Sheep Child" and "Falling" trap the reader in a haunting, if inexpressible, certainty that a much larger, grander, demonic world— compounded of Heaven and Hell—lies just the other side of the limits of his known, calculable existence. and it waits, like the dead, for him to step inside:

> I woke, dying,
>
>> In the summer sun of the hillside, with my eyes
>> Far more than human. I saw for a blazing moment
>> The great grassy world from both sides,
>> Man and beast in the round of their need,
>> And the hill wind stirred in my wool,
>> My hoof and my hand clasped each other,
>> I ate my one meal
>> Of milk, and died
>> Staring . . .

The reader must be willing to drown, fly, burn with a flame that sets all dreams on fire, and be the fire.

From "The Fiend" to "Falling," Dickey has been trying to find a medium that would enable him to *use* the maximum of his creative intelligence in poetry. To this end, he has chosen in "Falling" exactly the right subject and form. Both are moving toward a rhythm of experience that can sweep away all obstacles to realizing the fullest human potential: *"One cannot just fall just tumble screaming all that time one must use/ It."* When a woman's life-space has suddenly contracted into a few seconds, the necessity to conquer mental waste, to salvage every hidden, but discoverable shred of mental possibility, becomes absolute.

The opening sections of the poem stress the extent to which the girl's will, intention, participates in her experience. Her body and mind are both forced initially into reactions of powerful self-protective resistance, a mere reflex response to shock. But her will and creative imagination take on a larger and larger quotient of control. The female style of control is mixed with passivity, but the dynamic passivity of girding the body, sensually, as she "waits for something great to take/ Control of her." The beauty of healthy fulfilled physical life is Dickey's momentary stay against the chaos of the poem's life-crushing void. Within a moment of perfectly fulfilled physical being, her spirit lives an eternity.

The girl is strangely mated to air. The first half of her long erotic air-embrace is a turning inward. She is learning how to be, to be "in her/ Self." She masters "one after another of all the positions for love/ Making," and each position corresponds to a new tone or motion of being. The second half of her adventure is a going outward. She is no longer waiting to be taken hold of, but now *she* is the aggressor, who "must take up her body/ And fly." The shifts in her body-cycle—falling, floating, flying, falling—stand for consecutive stages in a being-cycle, rising, as she falls to her death, to a pinnacle of total self-realization. It is a movement from extreme self-love to extreme beyond-self love, a movement from being to becoming, from becoming to going beyond. Though her fall concludes with an auto-erotic orgasm, she connects, at the moment of climax, with the spirits of farm boys and girls below—there is a profound flow of being between them. This unobstructable river of feeling between the self and the world is the life-process to which Dickey ascribes ultimacy in his vision.

If ideas of rebirth and reincarnation are among the most compelling and pervasive in Dickey's art, the idea of resurrection by air—not water, earth, or fire—is the one that rises, finally, into apocalypse. A cursory glance at Dickey's biography might well support my hypothesis that, since the gravest spiritual losses to his manhood were incurred in air—via the incineration of women and children in the napalm bombings of Japan—he could be expected to seek compensatory gains to redeem himself, paradoxically, through that medium. In fact, he does achieve his most sustaining spiritual and poetic gains through the vision of air-genesis. It is my hope that in the years to come Dickey will return to the perplexing questions of war and race dealt with in "The Firebombing" and "Slave Quarters," and bring to his renewed treatment of those themes—surely the most troubling specters of our day—the larger generosity of spirit we find in the vision of "Falling" and "Power and Light." If there is a passion today that can counter balance all the hell in us, it is the ardor that fills these poems.

Chapter V

JAMES DICKEY, AMERICAN ROMANTIC:
An Appreciation
by Arthur Gregor

The sense of the sacred, fundamental in the great romantic tradition of Western literature but rare in contemporary American poetry, runs—like a beneficent river—through the body of James Dickey's work. It is this sense which gives his poetry its tone of reverence and other characteristic qualities. In many of his best poems ("The Owl King," "Walking On Water," "Armor," "Springer Mountain" among them) Dickey deals with the magic that results when the observer sees the supernatural expressed in nature, and experiences—is intimately involved in—this transformation.

The facets of the sacred—reverence, magic, and the terror that often follows a deep engagement with it—are qualities that distinguish James Dickey's work and set it apart in the contemporary scene. Rapture and terror, ecstasy over the beauty of the terrible and faith in the ultimate supremacy of light are the ranges of his essentially romantic vision. The calm, the firm classical structures that emerge when life is viewed from a level beyond the transformations—the transcended realm—are not his concerns. Rather it is the very process, the moving toward that assured calm beyond conflict, the transformation itself and its passions that Dickey is centered in. Nevertheless a certainty of a supreme and ultimate reality runs through all of Dickey's poems however ecstatic or violent their tone. In this passion and conviction he belongs firmly in the tradition of the great romantics from Coleridge to Dylan Thomas and Theodore Roethke, however different his manner and language.

In language, locale, and many of his attitudes and attributes Dickey is eminently American. A key term in describing his work is *energy*. It is energy, so characteristic of America, that is Dickey's means toward his spiritual end— energy more than philosophy or even religion. Beginning with poems in BUCKDANCER'S CHOICE (*The Shark's Parlor, The Fiend*), he developed a form for his poems to meet the demands of his own enormous energy. To control and contain it—one frequently has the feeling of words wanting to burst from lines and off the page—he had to find a style appropriate to the needs of his turbulent power, and did so with his brief phrases that give his more recent poems a short, sharp staccato beat within often long, always free-flowing lines that contain the intense pulse of his phrasings. This technique is employed strikingly in his long poem *May Day Sermon to the Women of Gilmer County, Georgia, by a Woman Preacher Leaving the Baptist Church*, and in his most recent book THE EYE-BEATERS, BLOOD, VICTORY, MADNESS, BUCKHEAD AND MERCY is used effectively in medium length and short poems as well (*Blood, Knock,* among others).

Dickey is distinctly American in other ways as well. His manner is that of the American male: forthright, gentle in a rough way, sexual and self-assertive more than sensual and reflective, boisterous rather than subtle in lyricism. The fabric of life that shaped him and is reflected in his work is southern. There is a deep identity with the human forces nurtured by family (how movingly he evokes the presence of his dead young brother in his earlier poems, of his parents and his own family), and behind his responses to the fundamental conflicts in life—of sex, love, and death—one senses a folk-heritage and the emotionalism, the fanatic gusto, of folk-religion.

But, endowed with a superior mind, Dickey transcends regionalism and his distinctly American attributes. Were his poetry chiefly a reflection of his energy, it would have the effect of a bulldozer overturning the emotions of his readers. Not at all. It does much more than that. Dickey employs his mind to more significant ends than a mere coming-on-strong. His mind is an instrument for an intelligence that derives from an intuitive power aimed at the "grand scheme."

Dickey sees the individual, human or animal, as part of a supreme network whose outline glimmers in the joys and sorrows, in the turmoil of the individual's life. With Emily Dickinson (and other poets of the great vision) he shares the conviction that "This world is not conclusion;/A sequel stands beyond." Invariably, his characters begin to participate in a grand order which is woven through their dreams and lives and is felt at odd moments. In the depth and terror of the dark hovers the angel of light. Again and again Dickey shows us that at the end of the visibles doomed to disappear hang the invisibles with their redemptive wings and in a glimmer of gold—a color, a symbol that recurs frequently, especially in his earlier work. Whether a young woman falls through space, bums awake in the gutter, couples make love in wrecked cars or motels; whether his people are lifeguards, hunters, pilots, members of his family, the sick or the well, he always touches upon the invisibles that surround them and make up the hidden stream of which they are a part. If Dickey's energy and psyche are American, his vision is not: it is one of man's spiritual reality and cosmic connection.

Thus James Dickey's work is affirmative. It belongs to the great tradition of romantic and visionary literature. It deals with the unchanging human dilemma in terms of the conditions of lives that are always changing. It is not hermetic, not at all; it is not privately self-indulgent, not ridden with ennui and the gloom of emptiness. It is not aggressive in a sociological sense; it does not seek to reform *per se*; it aims to evoke and reveal. It is never petty. It affirms the grandeur of life by coping with its conflicts with profound affection.

Arthur Gregor

Chapter VI

A NOTE ON MEANINGLESS BEING in "CHERRYLOG ROAD"
by William J. Martz

The poems of James Dickey typically express the primacy of being. He is readily recognized as a romantic poet, passionate intensity his hallmark. To live life with joy and depth is his persistent aim. Although his poems readily comprehend the darker side of things—anguish, suffering, despair—his affirmation, his joyous spirituality triumphs in the end.

"Cherrylog Road" is one of his best poems, or at least this is the assumption from which I am going to proceed. One might think that one of his best poems might also be one most representative of his work. And yet "Cherrylog Road" ends as a paradox of meaningless being. I mean "ends" in two senses, first as a statement of my interpretation of the total thematic effect of the poem, and secondly as a literal reference to the last stanza, in which the speaker concludes the story he is telling. He speaks in the past tense, but with the immediacy of the present. He is describing an incident in which he has just enjoyed sex in a junkyard, hops on his motorcycle, "a bicycle fleshed / With power," tears down Highway 106, is "drunk" on the wind and finds himself "Wringing the handlebar for speed, / Wild to be wreckage forever."

There is a strong suggestion of paradox in the phrase

"wreckage forever," which, as the poem works, sums up the total reaction of the young man to his experience. He has just had an experience that is incontestably temporary. He will probably never see Doris Holbrook again, and if he does it will be just for sex, that is, not for love, not for marriage, not for enduring relationship. It could, of course, be said that he simply feels guilty and wants, out of youthful inexperience *and* integrity, to suffer forever. But this is too formulaic to describe what the speaker feels. With Dickey *forever* means forever. The rhetoric points to a deep philosophic consideration, and, after all, the speaker in looking back on a past experience is in effect evaluating it. He knows how he felt then, so good that what he felt *ought* to be a permanent feature of his total Self. Yet, by implication of the temporariness of it all, so miserable that the experience logically ought to become just an episode, a stepping stone, as it were, in a long life. In effect the speaker is asking himself at the end of the poem why his maturing process could not have been more normal: sow some wild oats, become a man, mellow in maturity. But this speaker cannot escape his own being. The *forever* felt right after the escapade is part of his Self in the now. He is trapped by his own terms, is what he is. The paradox of *forever* is, then, forever anguish, forever joy. It is one thing for a romantic poet to comprehend the darker side of things, it is another for him to be torn apart by his own metaphysic.

The term *wreckage* carries similar paradox. Unless in the context of the poem *wreckage* comes to mean, ironically, something like "beautiful structure of being," it has to be taken to mean some state of being that is, at the least, less than wholly desirable. And yet the sheer exuberance of the closing line, with its "Wild" to be wreckage forever, surely suggests satisfaction with the state of being represented by the sexual episode. It is as if at the end of the poem the young man not only *flees* down the highway but is *directed* down it by the force of a mystical encounter in an automobile junkyard. He is directed by the experience, which wrecks him, to become wreckage himself. The paradox of *wreckage* is, then, anguished wreckage, joyous wreckage.

The poet, viewing his experience comfortably after the fact, knows that Doris Holbrook is part of his being, that the temporary relationship is ultimately permanent relationship, and this his permanent relationship with Doris Holbrook is, as a brute fact of reality, ultimately temporary. I was not surprised to learn that Doris Holbrook is not a fictional name. What made Dickey insist on using the real name? How silly, when adequate fictional names are available by the million. And yet, not so silly if one considers what the poem, finally, is saying. And not so silly, also, if one considers what the poem is finally *doing*, which is, to put it an old way, immortalizing Doris Holbrook. The poem, taken as a whole, is an act of love; there is no paradox about that.

Chapter VII

THE OPEN POEM IS A NOW POEM:
DICKEY'S MAY DAY SERMON
by Thomas O. Sloan

Life has passed judgment on James Dickey: he has been called "the hottest of emerging U.S. poets."[1] But *Life*'s critical accolades are always dubious honors—even when they are not disproved by *Time*. Anyway, to call a poet "hot" is surely ambiguous in this age of McLuhan. "Hot" in the McLuhan sense—spoken of a medium with high definition requiring only passive receptivity—is hardly the word to be applied to modern poetry generally, Dickey's poetry particularly. In fact, Dickey could be called a very "cool" poet: the printed versions of his later poems do not allow passive receptivity; though his words appear to the eye with the high definition of modern print, they march across the page with the grammatical obscurity of spontaneous speech literally transcribed. Here we may move toward my thesis. Dickey has

1. Paul O'Neil, "The Unlikeliest Poet," *Life*, LXI (July 22, 1966), 68.

From *Literature as Revolt and Revolt as Literature: Three Studies in The Rhetoric of Non-Oratorial Forms. The Proceedings of the Fourth Annual University of Minnesota Spring Symposium in Speech Communications, May 3, 1969.* Minneapolis. Reprinted by permission.

a deep sense of what speech, the spoken word, is. In his longest poem, it is speech which is both the agent of change in the poem's action and the poet's major rhetorical strategy.

I should like to begin my examination of this strategy by placing into perspective the visual implications of the term which Dickey himself has applied to his later poems.

Dickey calls his work "open" poems. The term may be a good one, for it may present to the mind's eye an image of an open area or a place where there are no barriers or at least easily transcendable ones. Indeed, "May Day Sermon" is about a breaking-down of barriers, including those imposed by rigid categories of thought. Its long title itself indicates that the speaker has left one category or confinement to address herself to a larger audience: "May Day Sermon to the Women of Gilmer County, Georgia, by a Woman Preacher Leaving the Baptist Church."[2]

Because it is a poem about "openness," it is a poem of revolt. Indeed, some of its first readers found it literally revolting. Soon after the poem first appeared in the *Atlantic* in April, 1967, a man who signed himself "the founder of the Poetry Society of New Hampshire" wrote a letter to the editor insisting that the *Atlantic* apologize to "the good people of the Baptist denomination as well as to the high art of poetry."[3] When barriers fall within this poem, reverberations apparently challenge the stability of other barriers as well, such as those between real and imaginary, literature and society, even (*pace* Misters Arnold and Eliot) poetry and religion. Some barriers in the establishment seem as susceptible to sound as the walls of Jericho.

2. I shall refer to the text of this poem as it appears in *Poems*, 1957-1967 by James Dickey (Middletown, 1967), pp. 3-13. For her invaluable assistance in explicating this poem I wish to express my gratitude to Mrs. Georgia Logan of the Department of Rhetoric, University of California, Berkeley.

3. See *Atlantic*, July, 1967, p. 26.

It is *sound* which brings down the barriers within the poem and which, for some people, sets off threatening echoes. Consequently, the visuality of "openness" cannot fully express what happens in this poem and how it happens—or, for that matter, to express what Dickey himself means by "openness." To realize what happens in this poem we must conceive of its experience in terms of something more than spatial analogies. After all, sound—particularly the sound of the spoken word—does not merely resonate through space, it affects our sense of time as well. These *spatial and temporal* effects cannot be compressed into simple visual models. I wish to take this argument several steps farther— into the realm where oral interpreters live: these effects, because they constitute a process or field of energy, are at odds with the effects of written language.

Writers such as H. L. Chaytor, McLuhan, and Walter Ong[4] have persuasively argued that it is difficult for us to understand the precise, creative nature of oral language so long as between the idea of it and its actuality falls the shadow of literacy. When we think of a word, we tend to think of it as a sequence of letters—linear, abstract, and objective, qualities inherent in the great orderly systems of thought which have produced modern ways of living and dying. Visual language scientizes speech. It anatomizes it, presents only its skeleton. Certainly it is true that from this

---

4. Chaytor was an early writer on this problem whose important work *From Script to Print* (Cambridge, England, 1945) was seminal. Marshall McLuhan's *The Gutenberg Galaxy* (Toronto, 1962) bears directly on the problem of print-orientation, as does his *Understanding Media* (New York, 1964). Of Father Ong's brilliant writings, from *Ramus, Method and the Decay of Dialogue* (Cambridge, Mass., 1958) to *The Presence of the Word* (New Haven, 1967), most reference will be made to the latest work, hereinafter referred to as *Presence*. I have also drawn heavily upon the ideas of Jack Goody and Ian Watt, "The Consequences of Literacy," *Comparative Studies in Society and History*, V (1963), 304-345.

skeleton the full body of the utterance may be reconstructed. But if McLuhan is right, many of us gave up the work of reconstruction and for generations preferred to wander among the dry bones of discourse. Some poets, like Blake, pointed the way out. But the major shift in our thinking about language did not come about until the new electronic media ushered in the post-Gutenberg era and began what may be the most significant revolution of our age.

Perhaps we should call Dickey's poem also a "now" poem. Like the "now" generation, it makes its presence felt. And it does this by being very much in with the current revolution in language—as I hope to show with this argument: *Dickey gives time and space the temporality and the fluidity of the spoken word.* The poem defies a silent perusal of its words on the printed page. It demands an oral reading. Once the printed page is translated into sound, the poem becomes what our vernacular calls "a going thing" or "a happening"—a process within which space is open, objects and images are changeable, and time is non-linear. Through the spoken word, the poem is made to happen *now*. The temporality of speech is the temporality of the "now," the present moment—both are most vividly realized at the instant when they are coming into existence, which is also the same instant when they cease to exist. When speech brings a world into existence, as in this poem, it makes objects after its own nature, fluid, in process of change and association. This world is by its nature "open." This strategy does violence to the "literacy" of our "literary" language. That other kind of violence, which pervades the images and actions of the poem, is a subject I shall return to later. The violence which demands our attention first is that defiant illiteracy which is Dickey's major rhetorical strategy.

Let us review Dickey's use of this strategy first in his own terms and then in the poem itself. The strategy was developed in his career, he tells us, in three stages. He realized, first, that a thin narrative thread woven into the fabric of a poem arouses a reader's curiosity, brings "into play his simple and fundamental interest in 'what happens next,' a curiosity that only narrative can supply and satisfy." Secondly, Dickey states, "I also discovered that I worked most fruitfully in cases in which there was no clear-cut distinction between what was actually happening and what was happening in the mind of a character in the poem. I meant to try to get a fusion of inner and outer states, of dream, fantasy, and illusion where everything partakes of the protagonist's mental processes and creates a single impression." The second idea disrupts the linearity of the first—for, as we shall see in this poem, the thin narrative thread is woven into a rich texture of sound that defies the inevitable past tense of narrative. "Everything" is to partake "of the protagonist's mental processes." And that means that whenever the protagonist is also the persona, the central speaker in the poem, everything is to partake of everything else. Not only time, but space barriers are to be crossed. In Dickey's work, these ideas led thirdly to the creation of what he calls "open" poems, poems that achieve "an optimum 'presentational immediacy,' a compulsiveness in the presentation of the matter of the poem that would cause the reader to forget literary judgments entirely and simply experience."[5] The final barriers to be crossed are the ones between the poet, the persona, the poem, and the reader. One is to be brought into the presence of the other, I believe, by means of the spoken word.

In turning now to "May Day Sermon" and speaking first of its temporal element, it will be useful to draw the distinction proposed by Robert Beloof, between *fictive* and *structural* time.[6] Fictive time is the time-in-the-story, the

5. James Dickey, "The Poet Turns on Himself," *Babel to Byzantium: Poets and Poetry Now* (New York, 1968), see esp. pp. 287, 290.

6. Robert Beloof, *The Performing Voice in Literature* (Boston, 1966), pp. 203-222.

time encompassed by past events which are narrated within a poetic structure. Structural time is the time it takes to read the poem aloud. Fictive time in "May Day Sermon" encompasses a few hours on a late evening in spring in Georgia. Reduced to its minimum details, this is the story the woman preacher tells: A poor backwoods farmer, a righteous, firm, even fierce believer in the Bible ("The Lord's own man," the preacher calls him), became incensed when he discovered that his daughter had a secret lover—a one-eyed young mechanic who would come to the farm on his motorcycle. Enraged, the father lashed his nude daughter to a post in the barn and beat her with a willow branch. The daughter's screams of defiance and pain filled the night. Later she rose from her bed and, seizing an axe and an ice-pick, drove the axe through the father's head and the ice-pick through one of his eyes. Then, moving to the barn, she set all the animals free. Gathering up all her clothes, though still nude herself, she joined her lover on his motorcycle and sped off into the night. So told, the story has the flat gruesomeness of a newspaper account, its potentially mythic features unredeemable even by the present-tense conventions of a headline. However, when woven into the woman preacher's sermon, the story is not simply retold. It is made to happen in the present moment. The fictive time becomes fused with the structural time.

The structural time of the poem is around 25 minutes—a not unusual length for a sermon, though perhaps a bit short for a Southern Baptist sermon. Yet the only meaningful way to conceive of the poem's structure is in terms of this structural time. I think we shall be misled if we endeavor to conceive of the poem's structure in even subtly visual terms—such as lines of uniform or corresponding lengths, a mosaic of metrical feet, rhyme schemes, stanza forms.[7] The

7. A host of essays have charged that our concepts of prosody are disturbingly visual and thus fall behind modern developments; to cite

poem's appearance on the page will upset our conventional expectations of how verse should *look*. It will drive the visually-trained grammarian wild. It will seem strange to any reader—except possibly those who have seen a literal transcription of *extemporaneous speech*. It will *sound* strange to all but those who have experienced the *fundamentalist sermon*—which is a sermon that is actually composed extemporaneously before the congregation and which is the most viable modern relic of ancient modes of oral composition.

The extemporaneous sermon—that homiletic method so abhorred by Anglican priests in the Counter-reformation—has precursors deep within primitive oral traditions. The monumental work of Milman Parry and Albert Lord has described for us the methods of composing poetry, particularly epic tales, in a preliterate age.[8] Some of these methods we may still see at work today in fundamentalist sermonizing: a speaker appears before an audience in a clearly definable role; he has a subject which he proceeds to develop orally by means of formulas and themes within a rhythmical structure determined in part by tradition and in part by the exigencies of oral performance before a "live" audience. The preacher, as we know, will begin with a text which he interprets—using his voice to free the Lord's word from the page. He expounds on the text, oftentimes freely ranging over a host of subjects, some of them only remotely related to each other or to the

---

two examples: Chad Walsh has an amusing account of his discovery, through reading aloud before college audiences, of the visualist tendencies of traditional poetry in "The Sound of Poetry in the Age of McLuhan," *Book World* of The Chicago *Tribune* (October 15, 1967), p. 6. Charles Olson's popular essay on "Projective Verse" is an attempt to articulate a program for "open" verse as opposed to "closed" verse, "that verse which print bred"; see Olson's essay in Donald M. Allen, *The New American Poetry* (New York, 1960), pp. 386-397.

8. Albert Lord's *The Singer of Tales* (Cambridge, Mass, 1960) advanced Parry's earlier research.

text, speaking as the spirit moves him. His formulas are addresses to the audience—"O, brethren! . . . O Christians! . . . Listen, my friends. . . ." His themes are commonplaces involved in expounding on a text; the most important of these commonplaces is the final exhortation to the congregation to come forward, to make a decision for Christ. The spirit moves the preacher between the text of the Lord's word and his congregation by means of these formulas and themes, from simplistic hermeneutics to rafter-ringing exhortations. The tradition and exigencies of oral performance before this audience are best conveyed by the fundamentalist churchmember's response to a satisfying sermon: "The preacher brought a good message." The source of the message is the spirit, the bringer of the word from God and efficient cause of the preacher's rhetoric.

Such is the structure of "May Day Sermon." The preacher has her congregation, but we are meant to believe it consists of all the women of Gilmer County. She has her text, the narrative just reviewed.[9] She creates her sermon, although this is not a Sunday morning sermon but a May Day Sermon and it is delivered outside the church. The speaking situation within which the poem "happens" is difficult to visualize because it is symbolic—as I shall discuss later, it is what all the actions and agents in the poem are in the process

---

9. I am tempted to compare this poem in this respect with Dickey's other long poem, "Falling," which first presents its "text"— part of the recent newsstory from the New York *Times* concerning an airline stewardess who fell to her death when an emergency door suddenly sprang open in midflight—and then expounds on the text in a style of extemporaneous speech similar to that in "May Day Sermon". However, the style does not seem to work in "Falling"—partly, I think, because the full use of the conventions of extemporaneous speech are not employed, are not, for that matter, even appropriate, but mostly because the persona seems only to be a disembodied voice. Even the generalized lyric voice when presenting the spoken word has to have a body. It has to resonate from some perceptible "interior" regardless of how diffuse and symbolic.

of becoming, a renewable force. Nonetheless, the situation is tangible enough for the poem to utilize the conventions of fundamentalist sermonizing. Although the preacher in this case is a woman—and even though the woman recognizes that she has performed a man's role in preaching—a woman preacher would not be considered unconventional in the fundamentalist church, which is, paradoxically, one of the most liberal in allowing women into the ministry.

Her formulas are addresses to her congregation: "Children," she says over and over again. "Listen . . . O sisters . . . O daughters . . ." And her formulas are also repeated phrases, images, motifs: "each year at this time," "I shall be telling you," "fog," "snake." Her themes are the telling of the story, the fulfillment of her "text," and the continuous exhortations to the women to "rise up"—to rise up and meet not the Eternal Bridegroom but the very real and earthy lover, to answer the call of the spirit that moves through all nature and renews itself each spring. These formulas and themes break up the linearity of the narrative. They make the poem seem discontinuous and freely associative, like impassioned speech, an effect enhanced by the accumulative movement of utterances such as

Listen   listen like females each year
In May   O glory   to the sound   the sound of your man gone wild
With love in the woods

Little wonder that the poem seems a jumble to those unused to *listening* for structure.

In the process of speech, time and space are not merely transformed but brought into a unique existence. Time in this poem can be conceived of as the fourth dimension of the poem's spatial objects. The woman preacher claims that each year at this time she will be speaking this sermon. She tells the story in the present tense—not even in the *virtual* present tense of narrative conventions, not recreating the story but creating it in the present and through it participating in the emotions and motivations of the daughter. She herself becomes a part of the force which prevades all life, which renews itself in time, and which challenges all barriers to its strength, including the most rigidly held categories of thought. The woman is leaving the Baptist Church—a movement in space which has its implications in time: her spoken word is leaving its container, and like the spoken word of ancient myths regains not merely its oracular qualities but that potential which it had "in the beginning" to create life.

Her word crosses barriers in space, blurring visual distinctions between images. All male images in the poem become fused, and so do all female images. The Lord, the Bible, God, the snake, the lover—these images flow into one another before our eyes, forming an almost overwhelming communion. The Lord gives men all the help they need to drag their daughters into barns. The Bible speaks like a father gone mad. Jehovah appears as a snake. The girl as she is being beaten seems to be dancing with God. The father, too, appears as a snake—his legs disappearing into the fog, his body "Lashing" on the floor where he is brought down by the axe. The snake with its cast-off skin, the lover's penis and its cast-off rubber, the fox hide stretched tight on the wall, the barn's center pole, nails in the wood and the throbs of lust in the flesh—all these images partake of each other. All are manifestations of a natural force—as proclaimed in a remarkable passage:

> Sisters, understand about men and sheaths:
> About nakedness: understand how butterflies, amazed pass out
> Of their natal silks   how the tight snake takes a great breath bursts
> Through himself and leaves himself behind   how a man casts finally
> Off everything that shields him from another   beholds his loins
> Shine with his children forever   burn with the very juice
> Of resurrection: such shining is how the spring creek comes
> Forth from its sunken rocks   it is how the trout foams and turns on
> Himself   heads upstream, breathing mist like water, for the cold
> Mountain of his birth   flowing   sliding in and through the ego-

manical sleep of gamecocks   shooting past a man with one new blind
Side   who feels his skinned penis rise like a fish through the dark
Woods, in a strange lifted-loving form   a snake about to burst
Through itself on May Day   and leave behind on the ground   still
Still   the shape of a fooled thing's body:

The daughter's mutilation of her father's corpse so that it becomes one-eyed like her lover seals the participation of all male images in each other.

All the female images in the poem represent the other side of the natural force which is drawn irresistibly into life at spring:

Listen: often a girl in the country,
Mostly sweating   mostly in spring, deep enough in the holy Bible
Belt, will feel her hair rise up   arms rise, and this not any wish
Of hers . . . .

The woman preacher herself is drawn. And as she tells the daughter's story, she screams and cries as she feels both her pain and her bliss. But in her role as preacher she has something of the man's role to perform, too. Thus at the first of the poem she casts herself into the image of the snake and participates with the father in beating the girl:

as she falls and rises,
Chained to a sapling like a tractor   WHIPPED for the wind in the
willow
Tree   WHIPPED for Bathsheba and David   WHIPPED for the woman
taken anywhere   anytime   WHIPPED for the virgin
sighing   bleeding
From her body   for the sap and green of the year   for her own
good
And evil . . . .

But it is the preacher's response as a woman that allows her to participate most fully in the life forces she actualizes through her speech.

The spirit of this life force is imaged by the fog, which rises from Nickajack Creek and appears at times as a road. It becomes, in fact, the road on which the lovers disappear at the end of the poem. This fog pervades the countryside,

sweeping through barn and house and across the boundaries
of the farm. Its whiteness, naturalness and freedom contrast
with the "black box" of the Bible. The farm, with its
boundaries, its animals in stalls and behind fences, its fierce
Lord, is "God's land," "the farm of God the father." Swept
with fog it becomes "the black/Bible's white swirling
ground."

But if this is the spirit which "giveth life," that which
takes life away are its opposites: as I have called them, the
containers. This is true of all spatial images in the poem,
including the contained word. "The letter killeth," Paul said.
Only the written or printed word has letters. The Lord's
word has no life when contained in the Bible—but when set
free it participates in the process of life:

> —each May you hear her father scream like God
> And King James as he flails   cuds richen   bulls chew themselves
>   whitefaced
> Deeper into their feed bags, and he cries something the Lord   cries
> Words! Words! Ah, when they leap   when they are let out of the
>   Bible's
> Black box   they whistle   they grab the nearest girl and do her
>   hair up
> For her lover in root-breaking chains   and she knows she was born
>   to hang
> In the middle of Gilmer County   to dance, on May Day, with holy
> Words all around her   with beasts with insects . . . .

Above all, the poem is an indictment of containers, restrictions, barriers—including organized religion. The father is like
the vindictive God of the Old Testament. And when he
speaks his voice is "like the Lord's voice trying to find a way
/ Outside the Bible." But even that word is confined to a set
text. Moreover, it is that word—specifically, a passage in
Obadiah—which when read aloud by the father gives the
daughter the "word" she had been waiting for to bring her
father down. Unlike those confined words, the poem
celebrates the *process* of life, and it uses words that are
themselves in process. Like extemporaneous sermonizing, the

poem uses a text and frees itself from the text. But unlike extemporaneous sermonizing, it *consciously* celebrates a participatory life accessible in and through all natural processes, like spontaneous speech. The pain of love-making, the preacher argues, is "life-/pain" which rises through the body "like the process that raised overhead" the willow—which is "uninjured" even though its branches were broken by the father to form a whip to beat the girl in his cruel parody of love-making. It is also like the process of the preacher's sermon—spontaneous but purposive, creating synthesis, participation, present actuality. The Lord belongs to the Bible, but there is yet another Word which is to be found outside:

> You cannot sleep with Jehovah
> Searching for what to be, on ground that has called Him from His
> Book:
> Shall He be the pain in the willow, or the copperhead's kingly riding
> In kudzu, growing with vines toward the cows   or the wild face
> working over
> A virgin, swarming like gnats   or the grass of the west field,
> bending
> East, to sweep into bags and turn brown   or shall He rise, white on
> white
> From Nickajack Creek as a road?

The final confrontation in the poem is between whatever is static and contained and whatever is in process and free. Because the confrontation is presented in speech—the spirit and the word—process and freedom are victorious, and barriers are broken in both space and time. The letter of the law of both God and man is broken. Yet because the speaker has so fully and freely participated she cannot condemn the daughter even for brutal murder. The daughter's action is tantamount to her own—a destruction of restraints. The father had set up his barn as an Ark of the Lord and took his daughter there to beat her in front of the animals for her sins. But even that container will not hold. The daughter sets the animals free. The preacher's last words are "the barn wanders

over the earth"—like Noah's Ark, but the animals are free. So
far as the preacher is concerned, the temporal confines of the
story itself are broken. The lovers disappear into the fog to
become part of that renewing life force to be celebrated by
the preacher "each year at this time." The lovers, the
preacher says, "entered my mouth your mind." Thus, the
preacher's word not only removes the wedge which separates
us from the past but also promises echoes into the future.
Such are the barrier-breaking reverberations of the word into
whose presence she seeks to bring her audience—and, we may
assume, Dickey seeks to bring us.

There is, finally, a more significant movement in the
structure of the poem than that between hermeneutics and
exhortation, between expounding on the story and directing
the congregation to accept the story's meaning. And that
movement is the woman preacher's movement toward the
happiness of total surrender—in her words, "Joy":

> joy like the speed of the body and rock-bottom
> Joy: joy by which the creek bed appeared to bear them out of the
> Bible
> 's farm . . . .

This emotion is, as it were, the proof of her case. The crude
humor in the poem, which serves as an ironic counterpart of
the violence and brutality, is a manifestation of her joy.

The woman preacher's speech is, then, a dramatization of
the poem's action. But thinking of the poem in dramatic
terms will short-circuit the poet's strategy in the creation of
her character. The poem is not a dramatic monologue. The
woman's character is not as clearly drawn as almost any
persona is in, say, one of Robert Browning's poems. She is
even less clearly drawn than Eliot's Tiresias—though the
male-female duality of her role makes that comparison
tempting. If we try to take her literally as a fundamentalist
preacher in a backwoods county in Georgia, we should find
her speech style improbable. She is less a person than a voice,

less a character than a kind of force—as she herself acknowledges at the end of the poem. Dickey's strategy here is to create a generalized persona, less in the manner of dramatic monologues and more in the manner of the traditional lyric voice. As he admits, his purpose is to "get a fusion of inner and outer states, of dream, fantasy, and illusion where everything partakes of the protagonist's mental processes and creates a single impression." The trappings of a specific locale, the conventions of extemporaneous sermonizing, the suggestion of a dramatic persona are all set in action through the process of speech. The argument that the preacher makes, that she and they and the action are all symbolic of the joy-giving, renewable life force, is proved by her own emotion—and will be confirmed by the reader, too, as he participates in that emotion.

I have been arguing that this poem should be of interest to us for the way in which it asserts the creative force of the spoken word, partly through reasserting the ancient values of oral composition. In our literate, typographical culture a word is not only something which happens in time but also something which inhabits space and, more than that, something which can be fixed in space in such a way that it can serve as a tool to record previously lived experience. But to understand Dickey's poem we need to think of a word less as something that records and more as something that happens. Of course, I am not arguing that Dickey's poem is an oral poem in the ancient meaning of the term. The poem is repeatable. Like a genuine revolutionary's, its voice will reverberate into the future. We have the printed record— though we will misapprehend if we mistake the printed record for the poem itself. In fact, our experience of the poem must lie in the tension between our literate responses to it as a repeatable object and our sense of it as a temporal event. The tension is analogous to the conflict within the poem's persona, the woman preacher, who sees the words of the Bible, who has read the law and the prophets, but who on the other hand is aware of the insistent, contrary reality of her immediate emotions. Moreover, I am not even arguing that Dickey's poem is unique in the annals of printed poetry. We have always had two kinds of printed poems: poems of statement, which are aimed at locking into time a clear-cut observation about human experience; and poems of happening, which have sought to pervade the present moment with a meaningful pattern of experience. The former exploit the solidity and permanence of print, the latter the fluidity and temporality of speech. Dickey's poem belongs to the latter type. But the way he accomplishes his happening should heighten our modern awareness of speech as an existential process in literature. If a poet wishes to be a *maker*, as his ancient name implies, rather than, say, a *writer*, then the burden is on him to find the strategy whereby we shall be kept from confusing the printed record with the poem itself. The strategy reasserted and modernized in our own era by James Joyce and Ezra Pound is the strategy of the spoken word, particularly as heard in *extemporaneous speech*. The continuing successful use of this strategy accounts in part for the strangeness, even the obscurity of much modern poetry— including "May Day Sermon".

My concern in this essay has been rhetorical, in exploring the connections between the poem and us by means of certain experienceable strategies. I realize that in making this search I have left many of the poem's details unexplored, most notably the details in which the poem reverberates with religious and sexual myths. The major rhetorical strategy which I have concentrated on is perhaps the most ancient and the most continuous of all creative strategies. Our religious myths give this strategy to God, the Divine Maker or Poet, who created the world by speaking. And, so far as we know, man's primary mode of intelligence, celebration, and magic has always been the strategy of speech, except for the brief period of its almost unrelieved subversion by print. This ancient strategy is also as once, paradoxically, the source of this poem's modernity and the rationale of its violence. One seems necessarily to partake of the other. Much modern poetry is outrageous, as this poem is, but purposefully so, and part of the outrage is committed against our conventional notions of literature, letters, writing. I am not suggesting that violence may be the true art of our age or that whatever poem is violent is ipso facto modern. I am suggesting that what is happening now may be related in an important way to our rediscovery of the spoken word, and that violence seems naturally a part of what is happening now, and that whatever poem realizes the participatory nature of the spoken word deserves our attention now.

Students of communication have described modern electronic media as extensions of man's voice, which have penetrated time and space and turned the world—in McLuhan's phrase—"into a vast global village." As Walter Ong states:

> Sound, bound to the present time by the fact that it exists only at the instant when it is going out of existence, advertises presentness. It heightens presence in the sense of the existential relationship of person to person (I am in your presence; you are present to me), with which our concept of present time (as against past and future) connects: present time is related to us as is a person whose presence we experience. It is "here." It envelops us. Even the voice of one dead, played from a recording, envelops us with his presence as no picture can. Our sense of global unity is thus due not merely to the fact that information now moves with near-instanteity across the globe. It is also due to the electronically implemented presence of the word as sound.[10]

Perhaps, then, the urgency of our position in time and space is caused not simply by the imminent threat of complete annihilation—that may be too horrible a prospect even to contemplate or to keep unrepressed—but also by the speed, immediacy, extension, in short the *presence* of man's

10. *Presence,* p. 101.

voice. Thanks to communication afforded to and by this voice, things can be made to happen everywhere now. A riot in Berkeley, Tokyo, Paris is seen and heard in Chicago, New York, London, within moments or at the most hours after it begins. The "now" generation has discovered that it can throw its voice even into remote deliberative bodies through the ventriloquism of violence. In fact, violent protest can now become the shout heard round the world. Perhaps some historian in the distant future will look back on our epoch as a time of world revolution abetted by modern communications media that paradoxically gave back to man his most primitive voice and restored to a complex technological society something of its gossipy small-town origins. Violence seems inevitably a method or an initial result of any great revolution.

But violence also shares one important attribute with the spoken word: it, too, can "heighten presence." *That* attribute of violence is, I think, more relevant to the "now" generation and to Dickey's poem than the others. The present generation is called a "now" generation not simply because it is present now but also because the past has so little relevance and the future seems so full of destructive certainties that the only significant time for existence can be *now*. The critic looks toward the past. The genuine revolutionary looks toward the future. The "now" generation seeks a way of living meaningfully in the present. Loving is one way. Violence is another. Both will break down barriers. Violence will break down the most insufferable barrier of all, anonymity. Moreover, it is not surprising that the rhetoric in modern protest utilizes methods akin to extemporaneous sermonizing. To scholars imbued with the methods of criticism, these protesting speakers seem anti-intellectual because they seem to convey no past sense, not even the "pastness" of having prepared to speak. When we turn to them as revolutionaries and ask the totally irrelevant question concerning their program for the future we receive the only relevant answer, the continued presence of violent protest.

Violence in Dickey's poem is inherently a part of the same kind of rhetoric—less nihilistic, perhaps, though no less existential and no less a part of the spoken word's field of energy. It is a way—perhaps a thoroughly modern way—whereby the poem creates the character of its presence and makes that presence felt through the action of breaking down barriers. It creates its presence through sound and in the process wreaks violence on our conventional notions of literary language. This violence is epitomized in the actions and images within the poem itself. On the other hand, the poem celebrates—in the way only the spoken word can celebrate—a renewing, ongoing life force by bringing us into the presence of that force. Its violence is the sound of categories crumbling. Its faith in the future is the promise of re-asserting its presence—less in the manner of violent protest than in the manner of a re-affirmable myth concerning the cyclical force of life.

Peter Davison has argued that James Dickey is one of the two major poets of our age—the other being Robert Lowell. Davison finds Dickey's success to lie partly in the achievement of "a method which would enable him to move backward and forward in time as well as space."[11] I should argue that Dickey discovered that method in his full realization of the resonance of the spoken word. Dickey's own measure of success, as he himself has described it, is the degree to which he gets the reader to participate in the poem. When "May Day Sermon" is read aloud, it places great demands on the performer but it leads inevitably to a kind of understanding possible only through reading aloud. The arrangement of the words on the page, the absence of traditional grammatical helps, the association of images, the violence—these suddenly make sense. Meanwhile the oral

11. Peter Davison, "The Difficulties of Being Major: the Poetry of Robert Lowell and James Dickey," *Atlantic* (October, 1967), p. 120.

reader is himself drawn into the power and energy of the poem. That, in part, is what this "new orality" in modern poetry is all about. But if what makes this poem so immediate, or relevant, or direct in its communication to us today is its "orality," that quality must be seen as an echo of the most ancient use of human speech: as a magical sound that creates presence.

Chapter VIII

James Dickey's DELIVERANCE:
Darkness Visible
by Daniel B. Marin

The maze is built up on the box's top and an arrowed path snakes through it around twenty or more penny-size holes bored into the floor of its roofless passages. Two control knobs that you turn to tilt the top protrude from adjacent sides of the walnut box, which is somewhat larger than a piece of typing paper and five inches deep. The game is one of several about the James Dickey household this relaxed Sunday afternoon—"The house is booby-trapped with games," he says. The object of this one is to coax a steel marble along the path through the maze, by tilting the top one way and another, without letting it drop into any of the holes. "Go on, try it," Dickey says grinning, rocking forward on his toes, delighted and genial. Even halfway is hard. Dickey's hands indicate, "Watch," and he hunches down over the box, focuses his fingers on the knobs, and squeezes all the

NOTE: All quotations from Dickey's poetry are from his most recent collection, *The Eye-Beaters, Blood, Victory, Madness, Buckhead and Mercy,* Doubleday and Company, Garden City, N. Y., 1970; all quotations from *Deliverance* are from the hard-cover edition (rather than from the *Atlantic Monthly* where part of it appeared), Houghton, Mifflin, Boston, 1970.

Daniel B. Marin, "James Dickey's *Deliverance*: Darkness Visible," *The South Carolina Review,* III (November 1970), 49-59. Reprinted by permission of *The South Carolina Review.*

finely balanced energy of his generous mind and body through the control knobs into the marble. It moves. Stops. Moves. Moves from beginning to end; then back out again from end to beginning. The fingers unfocus and spread, and the grin relaxes back out onto his face "in pure abandon."

Concentration, release, systole, diastole.

More than any man I have known, James Dickey senses and, in the gestures of his play and work, expresses the deepest rhythms of the mortal creaturely life which men share with all animal creation—with fish, snake, seal, lizard, horse, fox, dog, wolverine, sheep, tiger, butterfly, bird:

Heavy summer. Heavy. Companion, if we climb our mortal bodies
High with great effort, we shall find ourselves
Flying with the life
Of the birds of death. We have come up
Under buzzards   they face us

Slowly   slowly circling   and as we watch them they turn us
Around, and you and I spin
Slowly, slowly rounding
Out the hill. We are level
Exactly on this moment: exactly on the same bird-
plane with those deaths. They are the salvation of our sense
Of glorious movement. Brother, it is right for us to face
Them every which way, and come to ourselves and come
From every direction
There is. Whirl and stand fast!

Dickey touches that life truly and measures precisely its range of terrors and joys.

The terror of creaturely life is what Ed Gentry, central character and narrator of Dickey's first novel, discovers in other men and in himself, nearer the surface than the protective fat of his daily routine let him imagine. *Deliverance* is the ferocious tale of a weekend canoe ride Ed and three other city men take down a wild and glorious stretch of the Cahulawassee, a north Georgia river which will soon be dammed up, flooded into a lake, and made over by the real estate people "into," as Lewis Medlock, leader of the expedition, puts it, "one of their havens." But the trip turns into a gauntlet of violence and death that forces Ed to find in himself a cunning beast of prey that will stalk and kill its quarry: another man.

Though sometimes the ferocity recedes, the novel's tonal range never includes the "pure abandon" that is within the broader reach of Dickey's poetry, notably in his most recent collection, *The Eye-Beaters, Blood, Victory, Madness, Buckhead and Mercy.* Ed is driven to his discovery by violence, terror, and desperation, and his tale is, therefore, *un*relaxing. Even near the end, just after the canoe, carrying the three who are still alive, thrusts over a waterfall and pitches down six feet into, at last, calm water, we are not back safe.

What is left? Probably the trickiest and most crucial thing of all: deception, plausible deception. Without facing a full investigation, and likely more, they can't tell anyone what truly happened. How can they get back to their lives in the city? Ed invents an account that will get them through if they "don't mess up on the details." "Control, baby," says Ed. "It can be controlled." Indeed, for Ed's creator, as well as for Ed, unrelaxed control and credibility are the whole game.

Dickey's strategy in *this* game is to get the story told with tense and astonishing clarity that never lets us drop into doubt. As soon as Ed begins to speak, we attend—and believe:

> It unrolled slowly, forced to show its colors, curling and snapping back whenever one of us turned loose. The whole land was very tense until we put our four steins on its corners and laid the river out to run for us through the mountains 150 miles north. Lewis' hand took a pencil and marked out a small strong X in a place where some of the green bled away and the paper changed with high ground, and began to work downstream, northeast to southwest through the printed woods. I watched the hand rather than the location, for it seemed to have power over the terrain, and when it stopped for Lewis' voice to explain something, it was as though all streams everywhere quit running, hanging silently where they were to let the point be made. The pencil turned over and pretended

to sketch in with the eraser an area that must have been around fifty miles long, through which the river hooked and cramped.

First, there is the speed with which Ed gets to the central image of his tale: the river. Immediately we anticipate the trip; its direction is sharply marked out. And the map anticipates the land's and the river's energy, "curling and snapping back whenever one of us turned loose."

But there's something in the quality of Ed's voice, in his language, that pulls too: in the tensity of his phrasing ("forced to show its colors," "where the green bled away," "through which the river hooked and cramped"), in the bend toward fantasy ("it was as though all streams everywhere quit running, hanging silently where they were to let the point be made"), in the startling up-close sharpness of the focus ("I watched the hand rather than the location," "The pencil turned over and pretended to sketch"). What do you call it? A fineness? A nervous and scrupulous pressure? A something, at any rate, that presses the words down so exactly and tightly upon perception that not a breath is felt between language and thing: "forced to show its colors."

Through the eyes that Ed's voice gives us, the world suddenly appears as through fine, expensive binoculars, the kind with perfectly ground lenses coated to filter out all glare and let in only brilliantly undistorted light, or dark. Color and form turn to a foreshortened compactness more powerfully convincing than anything the naked eye feels even when it really is 7X closer. Look, as Lewis Medlock draws back some branches and we see the river the first time:

> The river opened and was there. It was gray-green, very clear and yet with a certain milkiness, too; it looked as though it would turn white and foam at rocks more easily than other water. It was about forty yards wide, and shallow, about two and a half or three feet deep. The bed was full of clean brown pebbles. We couldn't see very far upstream or down, but just watched the part in front of us going by and by carrying nothing, not even a twig, as it lay in the branches and leaves in

Lewis' arms. He let the limbs fall; they swept in gracefully and closed the river off again.

Dickey has said, "I tried to just concentrate on the action, on trying to tell an exciting story as simply as I could." (Quoted by Walter Clemons in "James Dickey, Novelist," *The New York Times Book Review*, March 22, 1970, p. 22.) And I think *Deliverance* is a novel of place and act more than of character. Most of Dickey's creative energy is concentrated into the thorough imagining of place and act, because, I guess, those put the heaviest pressure on the reader's belief. Image after image after image, scene after scene pushes into consciousness and memory. Rereading the novel you know things are coming which you'd rather not believe again. But the narrative drives you to them and forces you to believe once more: Bobby Trippe's scream of "pain and outrage" and then of "simple and wordless pain" as held at gunpoint by one mountaineer as he "melted forward and down . . . the arrow hanging down his back just below the neck." Dickey's strategy of presenting almost everything scenically with exhaustive insistence on details of immediate sense experience and of avoiding backing off into summary, except occasionally in the "Before" and "After" sections which deal with city life, could not be sounder, nor more compelling.

Characterization, on the other hand, is done quickly and deftly with straight, heavy strokes, as it should be in a novel of this kind. Dickey has a careful eye for the proper proportions here. By the end of the first chapter, the characters have been clearly and almost completely established. Thereafter, with the exception of Ed, they change very little. And in every case their actions are rigorously within the range of possibility and probability that has been defined for them. This is as crucial to the novel's credibility and sharpness of focus as is the detailing of place and act.

Ed Gentry is the most "rounded." He speaks of himself—

and of the other characters—with an engaging directness akin
to that of Melville's narrator in "Bartleby the Scrivener." Ed
is art director and half-owner of a modest graphics studio. His
attitude toward his work is largely representative of his
orientation to his life.

> For we had grooved, modestly, as a studio. I knew it and
> was glad of it; I had no wish to surpass our limitations, or to
> provide a home for geniuses on their way to the Whitney or to
> suicide. I knew that our luck was good and would probably
> hold; that our success was due mainly to the lack of graphic
> sophistication in the area. What we had, we could handle, and
> we were in a general business situation that provided for
> everybody pretty well, even those shading down toward
> incompetence, so long as they were earnest and on time. The
> larger agencies in the city and the local branches of the really
> big New York and Chicago agencies didn't give us much work.
> We made a halfhearted pitch for some of it, but when they
> were not enthusiastic we—or at least Thad and I—were happy
> to take up where we had been. The agencies we liked and
> understood best were those which were most like us—those
> that were not pressing, that were taking care of their people.
> We worked on small local accounts—banks, jewelry stores,
> supermarkets, radio stations, bakeries, textile mills. We would
> ride with these.

Ed must admit he is a part of this world, which he has done
much to create. Harmony is what he likes in his work, and,
we might suppose, in his personal life. In women he looks for
the "absolutely personal connection," and, he tells us, when
he "found a genuine form of it, small but steady," he married
it. Up to a point he is, like the narrator of Melville's tale, an
"eminently *safe* man."

But only up to a point. There are times when the habits
and routines of his life frighten him, when he knows "that if
[he] managed to get up, through the enormous weight of
lassitude, [he] would still move to the water cooler or speak
to Jack Waskow or Thad, with a sense of being someone else,
some poor fool who lives unobserved and impotent as a
ghost, going through the only motions it has." He feels

imprisoned by what he has created. Hence, perhaps, the attraction of his friend Lewis' mystiques: flycasting, archery, weight lifting, spelunking, and now canoeing. In short, there is a mild, though important, ambivalence in Ed. He tells us that when he woke on the morning they were to depart and remembered he was going with Lewis, "the routine I was used to pulled at me, but something in me rose daringly above it, full of fear and feeling weak and incompetent but excited."

The other characters are less complicated, at least as they exist in Ed's mind. Each, in pure and extreme form, represents an aspect of Ed's character. Lewis Medlock is restless, obsessive, and daring in whatever he does; but his daring is often rash. On the way to the river he gets lost, plunging wildly down country roads he does not know. Bobby Trippe, on the other hand, is fearful and physically weak and incompetent, though "a pleasant surface human being." His moment of rage was "like the rage of a weak king." Drew Ballinger is a sane, quiet, steady man, loyal to the routines that heretofore have guarded his life. While Lewis drives madly along roads he doesn't know, Drew follows someone who does know them. Through "sheer devotion" Drew has learned to play the guitar and banjo, but his devotion is far from the restless obsessions of Lewis.

The point is that by reliefing the roundness of Ed against the flatness of Lewis, Bobby, and Drew, Dickey has maintained the sharp narrative focus.

The focus is on what the river and its environs do to Ed. Ed's journey, like those of Marlow in Conrad's *The Heart of Darkness* and Brown in Hawthorne's "Young Goodman Brown," is into an unknown and repressed area below or out beyond that of the daytime-sunlight human consciousness. The general human sinfulness that Brown discovers in the forest so burdens his consciousness that he never really gets back into the sunlight again but becomes "a stern, a sad, a darkly meditative, a distrustful, if not a desperate man

. . .from the night of that fearful dream." Marlow can return from the horror of Kurtz's fierce disintegration only with a lie, because truth "would have been too dark—too dark altogether." Ed, too, can get back only with a lie. And though Ed's lie is, on one level, a matter of practicality and expediency, on another it is as moral a lie as Marlow's, for an animal of savage cunning that Ed hasn't known was there has thrust up from down inside him into consciousness and memory. Something terrible was pushed out and got free in that "land of impossibility," something Ed and we would rather not believe.

The progress of its emergence is even clearer and more real than Lewis' map. We will trace its route.

At the beginning of the "September 14th" section, Ed says,

> There was something about me that usually kept me from dreaming, or maybe kept me from remembering what I had dreamed; I was either awake or dead, and I always came back slowly. I had the feeling that if it were perfectly quiet, if I could hear nothing, I would never wake up. Something in the world had to pull me back, for every night I went down deep, and if I had any sensation during sleep, it was of going deeper and deeper, trying to reach a point, a line or border.

He has the same feeling as they embark on the river:

> A slow force took hold of us; the bank began to go backward. I felt the complicated urgency of the current, like a thing made of many threads being pulled, and with this came the feeling I always had at the moment of losing consciousness at night, going toward something unknown that I could not avoid, but from which I would return.

Their first night out, as Ed lies in his sleeping bag thinking, we move closer to that "line or border."

> I could hear the river running at my feet, and behind my head the woods were unimaginably dense and dark; there was nothing in them that knew me. There were creatures with one forepaw lifted, not wanting yet to put the other down on a dry leaf, for fear of the sound. There were the eyes made for

> seeing in this blackness; I opened my eyes and saw the dark in all its original color. In it I saw Martha's back heaving and working and dissolving into the studio, where he had finally decided that the photographs we had taken were no good and had asked the model back. We had also gone ahead with the Kitts' sales manager's idea to make the ad like the Coppertone scene of the little girl and the dog. There was Wilma holding the cat and forcing its claws out of its pads and fastening them into the back of the girl's panties. There was Thad; there was I. The panties stretched, the cat pulled, trying to get its claws out of the artificial silk, and then all at once leapt and clawed the girl's buttocks. She screamed, the room erupted with panic, she slung the cat round and round, a little orange concretion of pure horror, still hanging by one paw from the girl's panties, pulling them down, clawing and spitting in the middle of the air, raking the girl's buttocks and her leg-backs. I was paralyzed. Nobody moved to do anything. The girl screamed and cavorted, reaching behind her.

Now it is Friday night. On Thursday in "the bright hardship of the lights" of the graphics studio, a very different scene was played with the model—a restrained scene. But now, in "the dark in all its original color," the elements of that first scene have erupted into paralyzing panic and "pure horror," nor can Ed re-harmonize them. He is somewhere he has never been before, where nothing knows him.

Yet, he has just set out; he is not all the way. As he lies there the fantastic panic and horror suddenly turn real.

> Something hit the top of the tent. I thought it was part of what I had been thinking, for the studio was no dream. I put out a hand. The material was humming like a sail. Something seemed to have hold of the top of the tent; the cloth was trembling in a huge grasp . . . The canvas was punctured there, and through it came one knuckle of a deformed fist, a long curving of claws that turned on themselves. Those are called talons, I said out loud.

It is as though the little metal owl which that morning woke Ed as the wind rang it against the bronze birds out on his patio, has suddenly emerged from the blackness as a true and terrifying owl. In that blackness Ed, "seeing everything," imagines himself hunting with the real owl: "I hunted with him as well as I could, there in my weightlessness. The woods burned in my head."

The imagined hunt is the prelude of real hunts to come. First, the following morning in a dense fog, Ed takes his bow and pretends to hunt a deer, but, he tells us, "hunting and pretending to hunt had come together and I could not tell them apart." This morning, Saturday, he misses his prey. Sunday morning, farther down the river, farther than ever beyond the daytime-sunlight consciousness, where he moves "cautiously, as much as [he] could like a creature who lived in a tree," he stalks and this time kills his prey—another man, another creature. On all fours he follows his victim's blood-trail: "There was no path into the woods where I was going. It was dark there, but I could see blood, and when I couldn't see it I could feel it, and, in some cases, smell it." He has reached the border; now he has to get back. How? With the cunning of the beast that has emerged from within him.

The structure of meaning in *Deliverance* is articulated chiefly by such images as I have been tracing. However, at one point in the "September 14th" section, Dickey forsakes this rhetorical strategy and uses a less subtle and, I think, less forceful method of defining the meaning and importance of the action. That point is the novel's weakest. Lewis and Ed talk, for about fifteen pages, as they are driving toward Oree where they plan to get on the river. Lewis does most of the talking. And though what he says is in character and is focused on the trip and the issue of survival, though what he says defines the possibilities and probabilities of the world of the hill people into which they are going, and hence prepares for and helps to make credible the subsequent action, still I think it unnecessarily slows down the pace and movement of the narrative, because these things are done more naturally and more forcefully elsewhere in the novel.

Lewis talks about how survival comes down to the fitness

of the body, "the one thing you can't fake," about the quality of life up in the hills "that wasn't out of touch with everything," about the hill people and how "they'll do what they want to do, no matter what . . . they don't think a whole lot about killing people," but if "one of them likes you he'll do anything in the world for you." He illustrates his point with a story of how he and Shad Mackey were "running Blackwell Creek" and got lost and a mountaineer Lew had meanwhile met sent his fifteen year old son out at night to find Shad and the boy went, without hesitation, found Shad where he lay with a broken leg, and brought him back. For Lewis this father-son relationship sums up the valuable qualities of life in the hills. Lewis tells other stories: about how he broke his ankle while fishing up in the hills and had to get back alone; and about old Tom McCaskill's going off into the woods to drink and holler. These last two stories foreshadow the danger and menace of the hill country and its people.

But aren't these things done better elsewhere, without diminishing the novel's characteristic narrative drive? Aren't the menace and beauty of the hill country foreshadowed in the description of the town of Oree and in the sequence with the old man and the albino boy at the garage there and in the sequence with the Griner brothers, whom the canoeists pay to drive the cars around to Aintry? Consider this description of the shed where Ed and Lewis find one of the Griner brothers.

> It was dark and iron-smelling, hot with the closed-in heat that brings the sweat out as though it had been waiting all over your body for the right signal. Anvils stood around or lay on their sides, and chains hung down, covered with coarse, deep grease. The air was full of hooks; there were sharp points everywhere—tools and nails and ripped-open rusty tin cans. Batteries stood on benches and on the floor, luminous and green, and through everything, out of the high roof, mostly, came this clanging hammering, meant to deafen and even

> blind. It was odd to be there, not yet seen, paining with the
> metal harshness in the half-dark.

This description, which is locked tightly into the novel's
narrative current, dramatizes Ed's sense of danger and threat
in the world he is entering. Furthermore, the "clanging
hammering" violently contrasts with the "lovely unimpeded
flowing" of the albino boy's banjo which we heard two pages
earlier. And together the two auditory images realize the hill
country's range of terror and beauty, its ambivalence.

Though the world of *Deliverance* is a world of terror and
violence, there are moments when it is also magically
beautiful. For instance, in the "sleepy and hookwormy and
ugly, and most of all, inconsequential" town of Oree, at the
"dusty filling station" with the old man who looks like a
"hillbilly in some badly cast movie, a character actor too
much in character to be believed," is the crazy-eyed,
demented, albino boy who can play the banjo so that
"through everything he played there was a lovely unimpeded
flowing that seemed endless." In this boy, whom they meet
before getting on the river, is a kind of preview of the river
itself: crazy and wild, but beautiful too. We see the river's
beauty, for example, during Ed's torturous climb as he pauses
to look down.

> The river had spread flat and filled with moonlight. It took
> up the whole space under me, bearing in the center of itself a
> long coiling image of light, a chill, bending flame. I must have
> been seventy-five or a hundred feet above it, hanging poised
> over some kind of inescapable glory, a bright pit.

There are several such passages in *Deliverance*; enough, I
think to earn for Ed, and for Dickey, the image of the river as
it finally rests in Ed's memory. By then the dam has been
finished, and that stretch of the river no longer really exists.
It is Ed's "private possession": "In me it still is, and will be
until I die, green, rocky, deep, fast, slow, and beautiful
beyond reality. I had a friend there who in a way had died
for me, and my enemy was there." The tone here at the end

is quiet and maybe even melancholy. I am reminded of
Coleridge's Wedding Guest: "A sadder and a wiser man / He
rose the morrow morn," though not exactly. Is it that the
note of "pure abandon" Dickey reaches so wonderfully in
the poetry can never be sung here in the dark light, in the
"darkness visible" of *Deliverance?* But I am free to read the
poetry too:

Over and around   grass banked and packed short and holding back
Water, we have been
Playing, my son, in pure abandon,
And we still are. We play, and play inside our play and play
Inside of that, where butterflies are increasing
The deeper we get

And lake-water ceases to strain. Ah, to play in a great field of light.

Chapter IX

WHATEVER HAPPENED TO THE POET-CRITIC?
by Richard James Calhoun

When James Dickey was Poetry Critic for the *Sewanee Review* the word was that he was a "hatchet man," a reviewer in a Southern tradition of writer-critics from Poe to Ransom, Tate, and Randall Jarrell. This was a tradition of polemics bordering on outrage, appropriate for writers outside the establishment, which was always Northern and usually traditional. But it does not take the reader of Dickey's *Babel to Byzantium** long to realize that the reports about Dickey were highly exaggerated. He does not have any of the critical battles of the Southern critic of the past to fight—the old battles against the Northern establishment, industrialism, science, and logical positivism. His main target is simply academicism, or what he called in his first volume of criticism, *The Suspect in Poetry*, "the university-cultivated garden poets," who, he attempted to show, were "suspect."

*Babel to Byzantium: Poets and Poetry Now. *By James Dickey*. New York: Farrar, Straus and Giroux, 1968.

Richard J. Calhoun, "Whatever Happened to the Poet-Critic?" *The Southern Literary Journal*, I (Autumn 1968), 75-88. Reprinted by permission of *The Southern Literary Journal*.

The "suspect" is poetry that displays the manipulation of language for its own sake by poets who are quite clearly intellectuals playing a sort of poetic game. If Dickey has a critical point of view, it is Dionysian, Whitmanesque, Lawrentian. The Southern element is his call for a rhetoric which communicates from poet to reader. Accordingly, the "suspect" are those poets who have forgotten how to communicate what they really feel.

In comparison with the early polemics of one of the elder statesmen of Southern criticism, Allen Tate, or with the attacks on the poetic establishment by Karl Shapiro, Dickey's critical debut seems pretty tame. The reader who likes to see ballooned reputations punctured may begin a Dickey review with high hopes that Dickey is just the man for the job; but by the time he reaches the end, he will find that what begins as shocking and unorthodox ends as something qualified, orthodox, even a bit self-contradictory. I hate to say it about the criticism of a poet with a reputation for self-confidence and with the rhetorical firepower to bring down established reputations; but, as a judicial critic, James Dickey manages to bag only Thom Gunn, James Merrill, Allen Ginsberg, and to wound, ever so slightly, Richard Wilbur. The truth of the matter is that James Dickey finds some good in almost everyone, even in poets he ought not to like.

Perhaps this generosity of soul is not all Dickey's fault. As a poet-critic writing in an age of professional critics, even a James Dickey must be apologetic. He seems to anticipate that most professional critics will dismiss any pretensions his reviews and essays have to being literary criticism on the grounds that his judgments lack a sound theoretical basis, and that his critical ideas are neither profound nor particularly original. Accordingly, Dickey sounds the proper note of humility in his preface, disclaiming that his book is a "full-scale critical performance" and admitting "that any reasonably good teacher of aesthetics could tear his 'ideas' apart with no trouble." Dickey is, of course, right. In our "age of criticism" he hardly seems more than an impressionist or latter-day Romantic in comparison with Northrop Frye or Murray Krieger. Everyone now knows that the "academic" critic can easily show himself far more knowledgeable about existentialism, language analysis, linguistics, depth psychology, and myth than the poet-critic. Randall Jarrell once complained that the attitude of critics today towards poets was that of a judge during a bacon-judging contest who would say to the pig, "Go away, pig! What do you know about bacon?" But René Wellek has recently pointed out that Jarrell's analogy was unfortunate, since this is literally true of the pig.

The poet-critic has definitely lost whatever charisma he once had. Yet the same charge of impressionism, of refusing to write criticism by the rules, that one might levy against James Dickey could be made against the criticism of T. S. Eliot in the 1920's, Allen Tate in the 1930's (recently it has been with a vengeance), and Randall Jarrell in the 1950's. But in the context in which each wrote, they were considered important critics because their criticism had consequences. In the 1920's and 1930's the poet-critic had an important role by default, because the scholars and aestheticians had avoided their responsibilities as critics of literature. The poets had to take up the task for themselves. Writing in 1920, Eliot declared that criticism by a poet was the only genuine criticism since the poet was "criticizing poetry in order to create." This was literally true. Eliot, Tate, Ransom, and others, were first of all "apologizing" for poetry in the traditional sense by defining its role in an age of science and also declaring a new tradition in poetry, the metaphysical-symbolist. Their criticism was almost as important a literary endeavor to them as their poetry.

But in the late 1950's even Eliot apparently recanted by repudiating in *On Poetry and Poets* his earlier claims for criticism, declaring that the poet-critic was naturally biased because he was always driven "to defend the kind of poetry he is writing." Today very few poets consider themselves critics. As far as the literary career of James Dickey is concerned, *Babel to Byzantium* is clearly not a major effort. His literary energies are devoted to his poetry, and we feel today that this is as it should be.

Now I am willing to admit that, judged as a volume of criticism by today's standards, *Babel to Byzantium* is merely a collection of occasional pieces, reviews, and introductions of the sort that a poet is asked to write nowadays. But I would also contend that it is not without unity or critical relevance to the poetry of the late 1950's down to the present. Perhaps I might be somewhat biased because I admit I share a cultural phenomenon of the 1960's that social historians have identified as a nostalgia for the 1920's and 1930's. My nostalgia is for that time when we looked upon our poets—Eliot, Ransom, Tate, and Warren—as our major critics. I happen to feel that in spite of their limitations, which we are now aware of, they revealed something about poets and poetry. I hate to use an overworked term, and I do so only because it is never applied to literary critics today, but the poet-critics of that time had a kind of charisma. As poets, they were doers who should know, even if they were not as systematic as aestheticians, who were just thinkers whose theory might, after all, be wrong. To their laymen readers if not to the literary historians, the poet-critics of that day seemed somehow to be in the position of the Secret in the Frost poem, "The Secret Sits."

> We dance round in a ring and suppose
> But the secret sits in the middle and knows.

One of the things we used to want from the poet-critics, in addition to the respectability they were giving to poetry, was rankings or judgings. We wanted answers in writing to one of the favorite questions asked of any poet after a reading: What poets do you regard as important? When Eliot told us that the metaphysicals were important poets, we believed him enough for his opinions to have consequences for modern poetry. When the New Critics defined the "tradition" for us, the foundations of literary history were shaken. When Randall Jarrell defended Frost and Whitman against the then-current views of their importance held by academic critics, his words had consequences. His volume, *Poetry and the Age*, became a kind of critical best seller, and our concept of the "tradition" was again modified.

My main disappointment with James Dickey is that he actually eschews this job of ranking, one that even René Wellek in a recent essay on critics allows the poet-critic.[1] Dickey's essays seem to promise reassessments, but his opinions turn out to be (except for undeveloped reservations about Wallace Stevens and Robert Lowell) as fashionable as those of any non-poet assistant professor of English who happens to teach modern poetry. Dickey likes Frost, Robinson, Roethke, E. E. Cummings, Marianne Moore, Howard Nemerov. I do not fault his taste, but I can hardly give him A-plus for originality.

Aside from this disappointment, I must give Dickey his due. His essays do have a certain importance in relation to the critical context in which they were written. *Babel to Byzantium* provides evidence that during the late 1950's and the 1960's, when Karl Shapiro and Randall Jarrell were carrying on the earlier fight of William Carlos Williams against academicism in poetry, against mythology, impersonality, and the objective correlative, almost unnoticed, James Dickey in the *Sewanee Review* was reciting his own version of the contention that contemporary poets were long on skill but short on substance of the kind that communicates a meaningful experience to a reader.

In those days, Dickey was not, however, quite as extreme

1. "The Poet as Critic, the Critic as Poet, the Poet-Critic," In *The Poet as Critic*, ed. Frederick P. W. McDowell (Evanston, 1967), pp. 92-107.

as even Karl Shapiro. He did not desire to overthrow the
Eliot-New Critical orthodoxy and replace it with anarchy. He
abhorred imitative or slavish following of tradition (what he
calls "the School of Charm") and tended to view poetic
composition as pretty much a powerful flow of images from
the memory or the unconscious. But he could not go along
with the woodland-wild calls for intuitive freedom from the
schools of Charles Olson and Allen Ginsberg; and he rejected
the poets in Donald M. Allen's *The New American Poetry,
1945-60* because they represented "the most unconvincing of
all poetic postures" and "posit a new poetic conformity-in-
anarchy. . . ." (p. 6)

Dickey agrees with W. H. Auden that the poetic
intelligence should function as a kind of "censor," as a
built-in critic which must determine "what shall and shall not
come into the poem." Consequently, as a critic, Dickey steers
only a little to the left of the middle of the road. His ideal
poet maintains a kind of poetic tension between the extremes
of freedom and restraint, between the passion of his visions
and the demands of language. He has discovered "a means by
which the intellect can function without inhibiting whatever
personal vision and imagination the writer may possess." (40)
Dickey's view of poetic composition is his own individualized
version of the old rage-for-order concept, but the order is
almost as important to him as the rage.

As a poet, Dickey has been accused of attempting to
promote a new cult of virility in poetry. Although he has
denied that such was his intention, he was seemingly flattered
by the accusation. There can be little doubt, however, that as
a critic he has intended to promulgate a cult of personality in
poetry, a new kind of profound subjectivity. For his most
cherished belief is that the good poem bears the stamp of the
poet's personality and not that of someone the poet happens
to be imitating. The poem may and should transcend the
experience of the poet's outer life, but it ought to be

produced out of a tension between the poet's inner life and his feel for language.

I have already suggested that Dickey's emphasis on subjectivity, on putting some sense of the poet back into the poem, is a contribution he made as a critic to the widespread revolt during the last ten or fifteen years against the Eliotian precepts of impersonality and the concept of the objective correlative. It was the so-called confessional poetry of Robert Lowell, W. D. Snodgrass, and Anne Sexton which spear-headed this revolt by placing a speaker, apparently the poet rather than a *persona* in everyday but nevertheless "extreme" situations. Dickey's own poetry and the poetry that he likes offer another version. Theodore Roethke would be the great exemplar for Dickey in his ability to identify the "I" with surrounding objects of symbolic importance to the speaker. Among younger poets, the recent poetry that parallels Dickey's view of the place of the poet in his poem is that of Louis Simpson, James Wright, W. S. Merwin, Robert Bly, and William Stafford. Theirs is a poetry of personality rather than impersonality, of a personality that includes the irrational, the unconscious, the dream. As in Dickey's own poetry the "I" is there, with an infinite capacity for extension, metamorphosis, even metempsychosis.

Dickey is concerned not only with restoring the poet to the poem but also with restoring substance as well as skill as a characteristic of contemporary poetry. Although he quite clearly regards these goals as two sides of the same coin, he is never quite explicit as to how either rather monumental task will be accomplished. There is a vagueness at the core of his critical terminology. When he talks about the "poet" in the poem he tends to talk in terms of distinctive "voice" and inner "vision." As to the former, he singles out the Frostian "voice" as "a technical triumph ... of the highest kind." (208) Every poet he likes, with the possible exception of W. S. Merwin, has in some degree established his own "voice." Frost, Robinson, Roethke, and Cummings have it; but an otherwise accomplished poet, William Meredith, lacks it.

"Voice" is important because it contributes to giving the poem substance by creating a kind of willing suspension of disbelief on the reader's part. When Dickey talks about meaning or "reality" in poetry, he seems to look in two directions. A poem has meaning if there is a proper relationship of the poem to the reader and also a proper relationship between the poem and the inner life of the poet. The poem has an element of the "real" about it if the poet is able to achieve a sense of intimacy between himself and his reading as an experience worth sharing. He will suspend his disbelief if he feels that behind the language there is "the presence of a living human being." (109) According to Dickey the real value of a poet's projecting a distinctive voice, as in the case of Frost, is that it "enables poems to come without being challenged into places in the conscious-ness of the 'average' reader that have seldom been visited before, and almost never by poems." (208)

Dickey also seems to be convinced that the reader's belief in the "reality" of the poem is coerced by the poet's ability to make "effective statements." Before he devised his own "split line," he became convinced that the simple declarative sentence is the basic unit on which poetic lines must be built. It was the composition of his early poem, "Sleeping Out at Easter," that showed him that "the simple declarative sentence . . . had exactly the qualities I wanted my lines of poetry to have." (287) What he found of value in his own poetry as communication, he singles out for praise in others. Theodore Roethke was the contemporary poet that Dickey worshipped this side of idolatry, and one of Roethke's signal traits was his ability to make "effective statements, ones you believe, and believe in, at first sight. . . ." (151)

If the ability to make effective statements is a criterion by which Dickey judges his fellow poets, a second is his belief that a distinctive voice should be reinforced by a "basis of narrative" that "described or depicted an action." (287) In his brief autobiography of his own mind as a poet, "The Poet Turns on Himself," Dickey writes vividly about the importance to his attempts at involving the reader in his poetry of a narrative in which "dream, hallucination, fantasy, the interaction of illusion and reality" are fused. (289) The narrative should quite clearly be taken out of the realm of the commonplace by the poet's "total commitment to both his vision and to the backbreaking craft of verse. . . ." (149)

Since Dickey deliberately abstains from employing the usual critical terminology, he never specifically refers to archetypes and says very little about symbols. He obviously believes, however, that there are images which are archetypal and essential if a poet is to relate his subjective world to an objective world of knowledge which the poet and reader can share. A staple of his own poetry is what he calls " 'the big basic forms'—rivers, mountains, woods, clouds, oceans. . . ." (291) But there are also what he calls "instant symbols," such as that created by William Carlos Williams in his poem, "The Yachts." Instant symbolization in poetry occurs at those "moments when a commonplace event or object is transfigured without warning, as though by common consent of observed and observer, and becomes for the perceiver both itself and its meaning." (244) It is through such forms, such images, that the poet is able to make at least part of his own inner life general.

"The Poet Turns on Himself" is the most instructive essay about Dickey's beliefs as to how a poet gets substance into his poetry, because here Dickey is simply using his own example to focus on a problem of ultimate concern to him as a poet and on what I regard as the central theme of *Babel to Byzantium* as a work of literary criticism—the relationship between the poem and the inner life of the poet. Dickey believes each poet has his own vision, his Byzantium. In order to achieve it, he is dependent on a flow of images coming up out of the depths of the memory and the subconscious, compelled by some personal necessity. He believes that his own best poetic efforts are the result of finding "some way to incarnate my best moments—those which in memory are most persistent and obsessive." (292) He seems to suggest that in the life of every artist there are what a critic of Thomas Wolfe has said Wolfe regarded as "privileged moments." Dickey calls them "intense episodes and events" in the life of the poet which "show us what he is and in a sense explain him." (281) He states his belief that if he were to chronologize his own poems they would explain him from what he *was* to what he *is*. Similarly, Roethke's poetry is that of "perpetual genesis, his own genesis." Roethke's stance, his posture as a poet, is "a cry of astonishment at finding the thing—tree, stone, shell, woman—*really* there, and himself also there at the same time. . . ." (150) E. E. Cummings's poems are the story of a man who displays a "jealous treasuring of his individuality, his uniqueness. . . ," relating it to our human ability to experience the "natural miracle" of "feeling with what we see, and seeing with what we feel, spontaneously, thoughtlessly, and totally." (106) Dickey's implicit argument is that the poet must use his talent, his command of language, to find the right words for his own vision—his Byzantium—among the many and confusing tongues of Babel. Behind Dickey's comments on language lurks a belief that there is an ideal expressive language which will reconcile all oppositions between vision and poem, poet and reader, if the poet can only find it.

It is subjects such as those I have enumerated, born of a subjective vision but related to an objective life which the reader can share, that Dickey believes modern poets need to utilize in order to communicate to their readers. The great poets of the century are, Dickey feels, Roethke, Rilke, and D. H. Lawrence, the "great Empathizers" and "Awakeners," who "can change your life not by telling but by showing, not from the outside but from within, by the lively and persistently mysterious means of inducing you to believe that you were *meant* to perceive and know things as Rilke, as

Lawrence, as Roethke present them." (149) Roethke's poems have real substance because they "make you remember and rejoice in Lawrence's magnificent little jotting: 'We don't exist unless we are deeply and sensually in touch with that which can be touched but not known.' " It is in passages of critical praise like these that Dickey comes closest to expressing what he demands of poetry.

The reviewers of Dickey's own poetry have been pretty much in accord that he is an affirmative poet, but he declares in *Babel to Byzantium* that he desires the tone of his own poems to reflect a "dual sense of being glad to be alive to write that particular poem and of outrage at the possibility of the loss of all the things that have meant much to him—outrage that these personal, valuable things could ever be definitely lost for anyone." (281) In his critical practice he admires a similar kind of tonal complexity in other poets. In reading Roethke, Dickey shudders from a characteristic "terrible tension not far from madness at times; not far from total despair, but not far from total joy." (151) In E. A. Robinson what Dickey focuses on as distinctive is "the desperately poised uncertainty" which gives his poems "compassion." (223) In E. E. Cummings what Dickey finds significant is a "half-comic, half-holy reconciliation with the events through which we live." (104)

What I have just described is the staple of Dickey's critical method. He makes no pretense of being a formalistic critic, explicating characteristic poems of the poets he examines, an enthusiastic impressionist like Randall Jarrell, who must quote to his reader what he enjoys himself, or a judicial critic and moralist like Yvor Winters, demonstrating how specific passages either show or fail to show the right amount of artistic control, as evidenced by rational content. Instead Dickey is content to define as accurately as he can the main subject, the characteristic posture of a poet, and then try to determine whether that poet has honestly sought to find the language necessary to express his particular vision.

If Dickey is in any degree a "moral critic" himself, it is because he characteristically applies the concepts of honesty and sincerity to a poet's performance. The honesty he demands is an honesty from the poet in confronting his own particular experience of reality, and the proof of his sincerity lies in the poet's ability to compel the reader's belief in the poem as an experience.

When Dickey stresses as part of his critical method the importance of approaching a work without preconceptions and when he singles out "presentational immediacy" as another distinguishing characteristic of good poetry, he sounds remotely like a phenomenologist. But the only classification possible for Dickey is exactly what he is—a poet who has been poetry reviewer for a little magazine, a writer of introductions, such as the one for Morton Zabel's edition of the *Selected Poems of Edwin Arlington Robinson*, and the writer of occasional essays. "Notes on the Decline of Outrage," written for the volume, *South: Modern Southern Literature in Its Cultural Setting* (1961), is an account of the tensions between his Southern past and the liberalism of his present, as he deliberately sits with the Negroes at the rear of an Atlanta bus. In 1968 it seems dated. "The Poet Turns on Himself" was written for Howard Nemerov's *Poets on Poetry*, and in my opinion it is one of the better and more honest essays on the creative process in that volume. The New York *Times* essay, "Barnstorming for Poetry," is one of the best and most humorous accounts of the poet struggling for money and reputation on the poetry circuit.

As a critic Dickey is clearly not a theorist, not an original thinker; but he is certainly his own man. What he cannot escape from is the influence of that predominant view of the poet in our time as a divided creature with a dissociated sensibility, which has come down to him from Hulme, Eliot, Tate and others. Dickey's version is a very simple one, yet central to all his reviews. Modern poetry has become so intellectual that poets have forgotten how to feel in their poems. They have become imitative and "suspect" as far as any reader who yearns to be moved by a poem is concerned. In reaction to traditional and academic poetry, Dickey may want to substitute some sort of total bodily response for intellectual pleasure as anti-intellectual as some of his reviewers have made him out to be. The way I read Dickey, he would simply like to restore a balance in modern poetry between technique and vision, substance and skill. Randall Jarrell wanted pretty much the same thing. The difference between the two was that Jarrell was more nearly satisfied with the commonplaces of reality than Dickey, who is on the side of visions, empathy, and transcendence.

In his recent essay on the subject, René Wellek concludes that the "union of the poet and critic is not always a happy one," for the poet always becomes suspicious of criticism as a science. But Wellek admits that we want to have poet-critics, perhaps as part of our general fear of specialists and of our desire for whole men. In my opinion Dickey's book shows both the negative and the positive sides of the poet-critic's performance. In defense of the negative side I would say that it is quite natural for the poet-critic to feel that he does not have to theorize about what poetry is. The attitude of a Tate or a Dickey on this point comes from neither ignorance nor arrogance. The poet's struggle with language is to *demonstrate* what a poem is. He is also a critic, as a by-product of his poetic talents, because there is a censor at work in his brain telling him what is good or bad in his own work. When he is asked to be a critic of the work of others, he simply applies his censor to their poetry.

The poet-critic may lack disinterestedness, as Eliot admitted; but at least he is a critic who can write, whose work can be read with enjoyment. In Dickey's case what he insists a poet should have—a distinctive voice—seems to me to be characteristic of his best criticism. In contrast with the great mass of faceless criticism we now read, *Babel to Byzantium* makes the reader aware of a self-confident but

engaging personality behind the words. The most idealistic
positive view of what the poet-critic can do is what Eliot used
to claim but now only Karl Shapiro seems to feel possible—
that he can write creative criticism, criticism as a work of art
in itself. I have always been a little suspicious of the concept
of creative criticism and especially of having writers like
Walter Pater quoted as examples. But even within the
limitations of the brevity of his reviews, Dickey shows flashes
of rhetoric which sum up a poet's posture in a way that could
hardly be stated much better. Since marking such passages
was one of my greatest pleasures in reading Dickey, I cannot
resist quoting some choice Dickeyisms. On Yvor Winters:

> Here in full force is the kind of writing by which Winters
> wishes to be remembered: the strict metrics, the hard, obvious
> rhymes, the hard-jawed assurance, the familiar humorless
> badgering tone, the tendency to logic-chop and moralize *about*
> instead of presenting, the iron-willed determination to come
> up with conclusions, to "understand" and pass definitive
> judgments no matter what. (183)

On Robert Graves:

> There are , some writers who reside permanently in the
> blind spot in one's eye. For me, that writer *par excellence* is
> Robert Graves. For all of his inescapable talk about the Muse,
> I cannot for the life of me think that he has ever had more
> than a distantly nodding acquaintance with her. (186)

On I. A. Richards:

> They are not by any means the work of a born poet, but
> rather the productions of a highly intelligent and dedicated
> bystander who has seen, late in life, that he holds a lifetime of
> poetic knowledge and information in his hands, and has
> wished to see what he could do with it on his own. This is
> understandable and commendable, and the difficult and
> modest successes of the poems are real successes. (180)

On J. V. Cunningham:

> Cunningham is a good, deliberately small and authentic
> poet, a man with tight lips, a good education, and his own
> agonies. His handsome little book should be read, and above

all by future Traditionalists and Compressors; he is their man.
(194)

On William Carlos Williams:

> William Carlos Williams is now dead, and that fact shakes
> one. Has any other poet in American history been so *actually*
> useful, usable, and influential? How many beginning writers
> took Williams as their model: were encouraged to write
> because . . . Well, if *that's* poetry, I believe I might be able to
> write it, too! (191)

In this vein only the late Randall Jarrell was competition
for Dickey. And it is with mention of Dickey on Jarrell that I
should like to conclude my own comments on Dickey. His
essay on Jarrell is perhaps Dickey's closest approach to the
unattainable ideal of creative criticism. I may be overstating
its value as a critical essay on Jarrell, but as a critical essay
per se, for its structure and style, it may become a kind of
classic—a sort of "J. Alfred Prufrock" of literary criticism.
Anyone weary of Murray Krieger or Northrop Frye might
turn to it for diversion. For the uninitiated, I should mention
that it is a dialogue between a critic's intellectual strictures
and a poet's emotional responsiveness. Structurally, it is
perhaps central in the present volume, a concrete example of
what is implicit in the structure of all Dickey's essays. For
James Dickey as poet-critic is often divided in his own mind
and contradictory in his views. In the Jarrell essay these
contradictions are the structure: poet and critic engage in a
dialogue in which intellect opposes emotion, criticism
threatens enjoyment. Dickey has dramatized the dilemma of
the poet-critic which is in part responsible for his own
contradictions.

Chapter X

FLYSWATTER AND GADFLY
by Richard Kostelanetz

One of the paradoxes of American literary culture today is this: while there are several first-rate drama critics, little interesting native theatre is produced; and although much good poetry has been published in the past few years, there are hardly any decent poetry critics. Too much of the poetry criticism one reads immediately betrays itself as puffing for friends, an underpaid form of advertising for which the "critic" usually hopes for some sort of compensation, and Robert Bly's combative statement on the dust-jacket of *The Suspect in Poetry* is not without some truth: "The older American critics, worshipping the past, write long volumes on Poetry and Original Sin, John Donne, or their own childhood, and then provide indiscriminately jacket blurbs for all contemporary poets." From time to time, one even hears of another much-published reviewer who makes a practice of praising every book he comes across, on the grounds that his services are "good for poetry." I have never read a book on his recommendation, nor do I know of anyone who has.

The Suspect in Poetry. By James Dickey. The Sixties Press, Madison, Minnesota, 1964.

To charges like these, some people retort that the state of criticism is irrelevant; but criticism does really matter, especially in poetry. Except by reading reviews, how else can one select, out of the multitude of collections published each year, the books he will read? Or discover poets with whose work one would not otherwise become familiar? More so than in any other art today, intelligent criticism becomes the major, if not the sole intermediary, between the artist and his audience.

In this book James Dickey emerges as unquestionably the finest critic of American poetry today. In a basic way, he is that sort of ideal reviewer every editor likes to have in his pages—the critic a reader immediately turns to when the latest issue of little magazine comes out of the mailbox, not because he is particularly agreeable, but because he has that quality we rather ineptly call "something to say." Dickey is gifted with the knack of turning a review into a significant essay, in which real ideas are stated, large-scale judgments are made, overall interests defined, analyzed, evaluated and questioned.

He also distinguishes himself by the obvious honesty with which he confronts his reviews. When he dislikes, the punches are not pulled; and he courts disagreement as a pesty fly does a swatter. On Anne Sexton: "The confessional quality of much recent verse, of which the works of Robert Lowell and W. D. Snodgrass are also cases in point, is giving rise to a new kind of orthodoxy, as tedious as the garden-and-picture gallery school of the forties and fifties." What prompts Dickey to be devastating is not, finally, the desire to be malicious, but honest fear and distaste; and nowhere else is this honesty more clearly present than in his 1955 review of Randall Jarrell's *Selected Poems*. Here Dickey opens by admitting his feelings are ambivalent and then splits himself into two critics, "A." and "B.", who argue against each other. At first, one suspects the device is just a gimmick or that Dickey is creating a pat antagonist, along the lines of C.

S. Lewis' Devil; but at the end, one realizes that Dickey really does have two divergent opinions of Jarrell and, as critic, he has cast his own ambivalence into a viable form. Indecision is an awful predicament for a critic to be in and an even worse one to admit, but Dickey is imaginative enough to turn his honesty to good use.

The Suspect in Poetry also manages another trick quite rare in collections of short reviews, to sustain a thesis throughout the book. What he calls the "Suspect" in poetry has "no relation to what the reader believes in as 'reality.' " Now, any claim to represent reality always excites my scepticism. Reality, as Harold Rosenbery once quipped, comes in fifty-seven different kinds of cans; and he added that one man's reality is a second man's fantasy is a third man's corn. Nonetheless, Dickey's notion of the "Suspect" takes on a certain validity in the course of the book, for he has a way in discussions of individual poets of taking certain rather glib metaphors that a reader had at first accepted and making him aware of their untruth: "Mrs. Sexton sees her stomach, after surgery, as being 'Laced up like a football / for the game' (as though footballs were laced up for games). . . ." Another example, too long to quote here, is his demolition of Thom Gunn's poem about the motorcyclists, "On the Move," on the grounds that the language's suggestions are irrelevant or wildly inappropriate. Every book he reviews he seems to read scrupulously, with a tough-minded intelligence; and although he damns the Yvor Winters school of poets for thinking that poems must express a clear idea, he still insists that poetry must make sense.

In the late fifties, Dickey, particularly as a critic, represented a middle ground between the academic on one side and the anti-academic "beat" on the other—a territory that stood, in general, for an engagement with the realities of social life and yet behind some of the classic virtues of poetic form; at best it was characterized by a synthesis of passion and intelligence. In retrospect, most of us see that out of this middle ground have emerged most of the best poets of the sixties—John Berryman, Robert Lowell, Theodore Roethke, Sylvia Plath, Kenneth Koch and William Stafford, to name a few. The fact that Dickey espoused this position in the past earns him more authority in dealing with the immediate present. However, while he may claim to be history's harbinger, his sense of modern poetry is still, curiously, too historical. In his preoccupation with poetry's content, he seems almost unaware of the revolutions in form that do, in fact, separate nineteenth-century poetry from modern, and this probably explains why he neglects to deal at all with those American poets who may be extending this tradition, such as John Ashberry and his school, and why he generally does not discuss how form may function in relation to content. In many ways, then, Dickey primes himself to emerge as an innocent, honest, clear-eyed boy from the provinces, rather than a sophisticated literary man; and this stance gives his comments a peculiarly one-sided quality.

Much of his critical brilliance stems from his prose, one of the most ebullient, engaging and incisive styles in American criticism; and like Leslie A. Fiedler's, which it somewhat resembles, it is capable of packing perception, wit, eloquence and argument into a single sentence. (Indeed, it is precisely this intensity, I would argue, which distinguishes American criticism from rather feeble English reviewing.) In his prose, food for a paragraph is shoved into a sentence; and paragraphs, which sometimes go on for pages, are just collections of sentences.

As a master of the short-short review (too often the fate for poetry), Dickey can concoct in one sentence a magnificently succint over-arching description:

> E. E. Cummings . . . is one of the most blatant sentimentalists, one of the most absurdly and grandly overemotional of poets, one of the flimsiest thinkers, and one of the truly irreplaceable sensibilities that we have known, with the blind, irreplaceable devotion to his exact perceptions, to his way of knowing and

doing and to his personal and incorruptible relation to the English language that an authentic poet must have.

Now, that is finely said, and very apt.

Like all wide-ranging critics, Dickey is able to encompass very diverse materials into a viable synthesis, and his scope includes not only poetry itself, but the literary business and social life as well:

> The pattern of introduction of works of this type [*Howl*] is familiar; they are offered as 'confession' with the warning (here by William Carlos Williams) that their authors have indeed 'descended into Hell' and come back with a marvellous and terrible truth to tell us. . . .

Again, it is "the reality" of things that becomes the crucial counter in Dickey's evaluation, and Philip Larkin, for one, is praised as "being in a continuously right and meaningful relation to his material." Incidentally, although the essay has little to do with the "suspect in poetry" [yet much to do with the related concern of questioning intellectual pieties], one wishes that the publishers had included, perhaps as an appendix, that essay called "Notes on the Decline of Rage" that Dickey contributed to the anthology *South* [Doubleday Dolphin, 1961]. It struck me, as a liberal Northerner, as the most intelligent and sympathetic presentation I know of the white liberal Southerner's ambivalent feelings toward rapid integration. Largely because the predicament and personal history were analyzed in depth, the essay has an honesty, and thus, a validity, that is rare in writings on the subject.)*

Although he is sceptical, Dickey does not find enthusiasm an uncomfortable posture, even when it is displayed on behalf of indubitably unfashionable poets:

> If there is such a thing as pure or crude imagination, [Kenneth] Patchen has it, or has had it. With it he has made twenty-five years of notes, in the form of scrappy, unsatisfactory, fragmentarily brilliant poems, for a single, unwritten

---

*It has since been reprinted in *From Babel to Byzantium* (1968).

cosmic work, which bears, at least in some of its parts, analogies to the prophetic books of Blake.

Like Jarrell, Dickey is among the few critics of poetry capable of humor, unusually stemming from a quick perception of an incongruous relation: "You would think . . . from the number of poets who attack Rimbaud's words as though they were *mana*, that he made his living writing epigraphs." Finally, he does not hesitate to quote at length, invariably with intelligence; and, to his credit, he eschews that stupid custom (or is it a law?) of obtaining the copyright holder's permission for each and every line he quotes.

A major trouble with *The Suspect in Poetry* is that Dickey is frequently much too nice to bad poets; and this generosity becomes particularly evident in his demolitions. Just after he finishes slaughtering a poet's work, he invariably reverses his field and turns up with something complimentary. For instance, after arguing, in no uncertain terms, that Charles Olson's "Maximus" is a thoroughly bad poem a result as much of clumsy and unoriginal theories as of overall ineptness, Dickey turns up with, "He has managed to write a few moderately interesting sections of long, unsuccessful poem which must have been the labor of years, and these are worth reading." Nearly every review ends on, as they say, an up-note, sometimes out of tune; and these reversals give Dickey an oafish image, which contrasts with the graceful ambivalence of the Jarrell essay. At base they probably symptomize Dickey's own uncertain feelings towards the critical position. On one hand, he seems a Southern gentleman, trying just too hard to be polite; and on the other, he expresses a certain sentimentality towards all those who write poetry. If the critic mentioned earlier believes that all poetry should be praised because indiscriminately kind words are good for poetry, Dickey believes that one should have a nice word for every poet, solely because the task of writing poetry in our time, in our culture, is so damn tough. Dickey writes that after experiencing all the blandness and aggressively anti-cultural atmosphere of American life, "to read even a dreadful poet like Tennessee Williams . . . or Allen Ginsberg, is to have one's eyes fill with tears." This attitude is somewhat justified (but does he need to be that nice?); yet I also suspect that at its base is a certain self-indulgence that Dickey expresses elsewhere. Because he slaves hard at writing and does not take adverse criticism too easily, he assumes that every other poet does too; and in making his own experience the norm, he inclines towards solipsism. Elsewhere, he writes, "Often at night, when I see that, indeed, the sky is a 'deep throw of stars,' I think of a poet named Kenneth Patchen who once told me that it is." Here Dickey hardly suspects that what is dear to him is terribly sentimental to another; to my taste, the metaphor is unrealistically homo-centric. Likewise, in his own verse, Dickey is not really tough enough, falling too easily into flaccidity and sentimentality.

Dickey probably sees himself as a poet who writes criticism; however, in the end I would reverse the order. I would sooner read and re-read a page of Dickey's prose than one of his poems (though I confess to reading both rather frequently). He is a truly distinguished critic, an advocate and exemplar of perception, discretion, honesty, seriousness, and intelligence; and that is more than enough to make him an irreplaceable force on the current scene.

Chapter XI

James Dickey: Comic Poet
by Robert W. Hill

Sometimes James Dickey talks too much, as in "May Day Sermon" or "Looking for the Buckhead Boys," but this fault comes directly out of what is good in him. For Dickey, life is moving and absolutely uncapturable; stasis is tragedy. One thinks of the copius and flowing Falstaff, whose life goes on forever in the power of effusive relationships; and when his love is abruptly fronted by rigid confinement of it, he dies, tragically. The comic Wife of Bath is pathetic in her declining years, but the going on, her pilgrimaging and wiving forever, is comic. In *Anatomy of Criticism*, Northrop Frye says that comic fortune often results in a new society precipitated by the comic hero and formed around him. Constance Rourke's *American Humor* suggests that the integration of cultures into a single culture is what is seen and recorded by comic writers. I suggest that comedy is more that which promises to go on; marriages are made, and fruitful continuance is implied.

Tragedies are about fatal containment. Despite such future-oriented resolutions as the establishment of Fortinbras at the end of *Hamlet*, that play is about Hamlet and the royal family's disaster, the disaster of the state in them. But it is a unique thing ended with them. There may be other tragedies, as those implied to come after the death of Beowulf, for example, but they are themselves. It is the sense of finality, delimitation of human activity, not just the matter of declining fortune, that is tragedy; it may not even concern society as a whole. Comedy is optimistic, openly affirming, not necessarily taking place within the societal framework noted by Frye, but within the individual. Thus we may talk of tragic poetry and comic poetry apart from their dramatic or moral qualities, or their societal relationships. Dickey is primarily a comic poet because he affirms copious and on-going life.

Paradoxically, Dickey has three poems about death that may be useful in trying to understand his comic vision: "The Lifeguard" (p. 51),[1] "The Performance" (p. 30), and "Falling" (p. 293). The first of these is about a lifeguard who tried but failed to save a drowning child. Late at night, solitary in a boathouse, he speaks of the other children who trusted him as they watched him dive again and again. The poem ends with a vision of the dead child out of the killing lake:

> He is one I do not remember
> Having ever seen in his life . . . .
>
> I wash the black mud from my hands.
> On a light given off by the grave
> I kneel in the quick of the moon
> At the heart of a distant forest
> And hold in my arms a child
> Of water, water, water.

This poem offers no expansive vision for its persona. One might claim that the lifeguard's life-sense has expanded in his new consciousness of death and guilt, but that would be to overlook the finality of the last two lines of the poem. The lifeguard is forever caught in that death-guilty moment, and the poem is tragic for its stasis in futility.

---

1. *Poems 1957-1967* (Middletown, Connecticut, 1967). All page references will be to this edition.

The other two death poems are of a different thematic order; they move in the direction of comic vision rather than tragic. "The Performance" tells the story of an amateur gymnast, a pilot in World War II's Pacific, who was captured by the Japanese and beheaded. Before his death, however, he "amazed" his "small captors" with "all his lean tricks." The climax of his performance was

> . . . the stand on his hands,
> Perfect, with his feet together,
> His head down, evenly breathing,
> As the sun poured up from the sea
>
> And the headsman broke down
> In a blaze of tears, in that light
> Of the thin, long human frame
> Upside down in its own strange joy,
> And, if some other one had not told him,
> Would have cut off the feet
>
> Instead of the head,
> And if Armstrong had not presently risen
> In kingly, round-shouldered attendance,
> And then knelt down in himself
> Beside his hacked, glittering grave, having done
> All things in this life that he could.

This is a poem about a man of good-will and free spirit who is decapitated. Yet I have had students to laugh, albeit nervously, when it was read aloud to them. Something of the finality of death is negated by Donald Armstrong's comic vision. His life is cut short, shall we pun, and we care very much that he is lost; but his story is one of abundant life, the excess that makes laughter and art. For Dickey it is particularly significant that Armstrong's affirmation is in terms of physical acts, and that by inverting his own body he inverts the fears of death into joys of life and the tragic into the comic.

From all that we know of him, Donald Armstrong always had the comic vision which allowed him to perform for his executioners, but this is not the case with the stewardess in

"Falling." The process of her fortune might be graphed like this:

(1) She is in relatively good fortune, alive and functioning in her tightly uniformed way; (2) her fortune suddenly collapses as she is blown out the door of the airplane; (3) she gradually, then more rapidly, grows aware of life, encompassing everything of her human world in recollection and hope—love, T.V.'s, lakes, skydiving, fields, fertility, mystery—rising infinitely beyond whatever "life" she had known before; and (4) she dies as a poetic fertility sacrifice and goddess, a tragic downturn which nonetheless maintains the girl on a higher plane of fortune than her former stiff existence: she becomes a life symbol.

"Falling" is an especially important poem because it exemplifies the integrative consciousness that Dickey identifies as good, and that we have designated as comic. In the epigraph we read that the stewardess is twenty-nine, the cruelest loss-of-youth age, and the poem plays on her being bound up, lacking the freedom and effusiveness of youth. She "moves in her slim tailored / Uniform," and when she falls, "Still neat lipsticked stockinged girdled by regulation her hat / Still on . . . ," we are set up by the poet for the loosening of garments that indicates her return to good natural things later in the poem. She soon finds that her body is "maneuverable," and we are told of "her / Self in low body-whistling wrapped intensely in all her dark dance-weight / Coming down from a marvellous leap . . . ." But the acute physical sense of her falling quickly fuses with the symbolic structuring of the theme of fertility. She falls "with the delaying, dumfounding ease / Of a dream of being drawn like endless moonlight to the harvest soil . . . ." As she hurtles toward the death that earth holds for her, her mind fills with life images: birds, woods, fields, water. She even comes to believe that if she could soar to a lake and hit it just right ("there is time to perfect all the fine / Points of diving"), she would emerge "healthily dripping / And be handed a Coca-Cola . . . ." She has already been linked symbolically with the crescent fertility moon, and this slant reference to Coca-Cola's exploitation of Astarte foreshadows the sacrifice to the fields that the stewardess will become.

By the time she must face death without hope, the stewardess has attained a sense of life's breadth that would make her an integrative, comic visionary, if she were to live. But she cannot, and in her new knowledge of nature she escapes the unassailable single terror of hysteria; she chooses the ritual of her death:

> Do something with water   fly to it   fall in it   drink it   rise
> From it   but there is none left upon earth   the clouds have
>   drunk it back
> The plants have sucked it down   there are standing toward
>   her only
> The common fields of death   she comes back from flying
>   to falling
> Returns to a powerful cry   the silent scream with which
>   she blew down
> The coupled door of the airliner   nearly   nearly losing hold
> Of what she has done   remembers   remembers the shape at
>   the heart
> Of cloud   fashionably swirling   remembers she still has time
>   to die
> Beyond explanation . . . .

She removes her clothes, desiring to strike the earth with as much of its naturalness as she can will to herself. The poem reverberates with the union of her, the earth, and the blood-mystical farmers on the ground who await "the greatest thing that ever came to Kansas":

> Her last superhuman act   the last slow careful passing of her hands
> All over her unharmed body   desired by every sleeper in his dream:
> Boys finding for the first time their loins filled with heart's blood
> Widowed farmers whose hands float under light covers to find
>   themselves
> Arisen at sunrise   the splendid position of blood unearthly drawn
> Toward clouds . . . .

She is almost apotheosized at this moment, the falling goddess of fertility come to astound her cult with her death:

> . . . All those who find her impressed
> In the soft loam   gone down   driven well into the image of her body
> The furrows for miles flowing in upon her where she lies very deep
> In her mortal outline   in the earth as it is in cloud   can tell nothing
> But that she is there   inexplicable   unquestionable   and remember
> That something broke in them as well   and began to live and die more
> When they walked for no reason into their fields to where the whole
>   earth
> Caught her . . . .

Obviously, "Falling" is not a completely comic poem, but in the stewardess' expansive vision—her creative identity with the natural world—we can see Dickey's comic impulse at work. In this poem he counterposes an inherently tragic narrative and the comic sense of fertile continuance. The stewardess is ultimately important to us, not because she dies so strangely, but because she comes alive as she falls.

Up to this point, we have not discussed the essential quality—joy—that distinguishes Dickey's unadulteratedly comic poems. Works like "The Heaven of Animals" (p. 59), "Encounter in the Cage Country" (p. 274), "Cherrylog Road" (p. 134), and "Power and Light" (p. 256) are fully optimistic, effusive with natural potentials, joyous.

The Dantean comic end, a heaven for people, does not enter into Dickey's poetry. It might be that it carries for him (out of a Southern Bible Belt culture) connotations of spiritual fixedness—a tragedy for human creatures. Besides, what he has called his "religion of sticks and stones" would be antithetical to any traditional Christian notions of immortality and divine reward. So he writes of "The Heaven of Animals," a cyclical living and dying that allows ideal participation of the living individual in the most profound processes of nature. Joy for the physical creature is to fulfill his sensuous natural self:

> Here they are. The soft eyes open.
> If they have lived in a wood
> It is a wood.
> If they have lived on plains
> It is grass rolling
> Under their feet forever . . . .

One suspects that Dickey is much more sensitive to the savage bliss of the predatory cats in this poem than to the fearless acquiescence of the hunted. But because of the restrictions of the *tour de force*, he does portray a kind of saintly victimage at the end:

> Their reward: to walk
>
> Under such trees in full knowledge
> Of what is in glory above them,
> And to feel no fear,
> But acceptance, compliance.
> Fulfilling themselves without pain
>
> At the cycle's center,
> They tremble, they walk
> Under the tree,
> They fall, they are torn,
> They rise, they walk again.

There is, nonetheless a fakery about this poem that seems to come from Dickey's discomfort in the presence of the Ideal. He is a poet of process, of the imperfection of human and non-human nature; he believes in an ongoing life force that "seems to promise immortality to life, but destruction to beings," as Melville has put it (*Mardi*, LXIX). Dickey sees joy in the animals' heaven, and he wants the poem to show his belief in integrative nature; but he deserts his position on the side of nature when he removes pain from the prey's experience. This is a very neat poem; however, in straining after its point it misses the profundity of real experience.

A much more real thing happens in "Encounter in the Cage Country."[2] Dickey (it is difficult to speak of "the persona," since it is so plainly Dickey himself) explores a very complex set of responses. At one level he is egocentric, asserting his human superiority over this beast:

> Among the crowd, he found me
> Out   and dropped his bloody snack . . . .
>
> . . . we saw he was watching only
> Me. I knew the stage was set, and I began
> To perform . . . .

He is playing a role, but not so much for the cat as for the spectators who have gathered for his display of American tourism: ". . . at one brilliant move / I made as though drawing a gun from my hip- / bone . . . ." He imagines having great power over the crowd as well as over the panther: ". . . the bite-sized children broke / Up   changing their concept of laughter . . . ." At another level, however, he believes that he is communicating with the animal, thus affirming their kinship. Unlike the "sophisticated," superior human being before him, the black panther is not fooling:

> But none of this changed his eyes, or changed
> My green glasses. Alert, attentive,
> He waited for what I could give him:
>
> My moves   my throat   my wildest love,
> The eyes behind my eyes . . . .

The man has found confirmation for his instinctual life in the eyes of a caged beast; he has drawn power that is deeply

---

2. At public readings, Dickey likes to tell of how he actually met the black panther at the London Zoo; the experience is obviously dear to him.

known and inexplicably communicable: "... the crowd /
Quailed from me and I was inside and out / of myself . . . ."
   The poem is comic in two ways: it asserts the natural
union of human beings and other animals, and it is funny.
Laurence Lieberman makes reference to the latter, saying,
"While the humor enhances the seriousness of the exchange
between man and beast, it also balances the terror as the
poem rises to a peak of spiritual transcendence." With regard
to the former, he notes a shift in attitude from Dickey's
earlier animal poems: " . . . he no longer transforms into a
new, wholly other being; instead, he intensifies and deepens
the human self by adding animal powers to it."[3] These two
observations are of the essence of Dickey's comic vision. It
cannot merely exclude the terrible; an expansive vision must
have room for the sprawling human potential and the fatal
constrictions of circumstance. And it all must end in
affirmation—joy at being alive. "Encounter in the Cage
Country" ends with the poet's knowing that he is uniquely
human, separate, and yet not unknown to the almost
mystical life force:

> . . . something was given a life-
> mission to say to me hungrily over
>
> And over and over *your moves are exactly right*
> *For a few things in this world: we know you*
> *When you come, Green Eyes, Green Eyes.*

"Cherrylog Road" and "Power and Light" are more
exclusively human poems. Especially in "Cherrylog Road,"
Dickey relies on the vitality of common people to approach
the comic vision. The nature-force that he writes about is the
sexual urge of youngsters from the country. The occasion of
the plot is a lovers' tryst in a junkyard. The girl has to slip
away from her frightening father on the pretext of stealing
parts off the junked cars:

---

3. Laurence Lieberman, intro. *The Achievement of James Dickey*
(Glenview, Illinois: Scott, Foresman, 1968), p. 21.

> I popped with sweat as I thought
> I heard Doris Holbrook scrape
> Like a mouse in the southern-state sun
> That was eating the paint in blisters
> From a hundred car tops and hoods.
> She was tapping like code,
> Loosening the screws,
> Carrying off headlights,
> Sparkplugs, bumpers
> Cracked mirrors and gear-knobs,
> Getting ready, already,
> To go back with something to show
>
> Other than her lips' new trembling . . . .

The quality of Dickey's humor here is not strained; the funny things in this poem come from exuberance—extravagant images that might very well have occurred to a boy who could rendezvous in such a wildly imaginative place. His fear of Doris' father is funny with the fears of youth, although there is no reason to doubt that the red-haired man might wait

> In a bootlegger's roasting car
> With a string-triggered 12-gauge shotgun
> To blast the breath from the air. . . .

The scene intrudes upon the youthfully serious passion with an irreverence that does not slow the two lovers at all:

> . . . we clung, glued together,
> With the hooks of the seat springs
> Working through to catch us red-handed
> Amidst the gray breathless batting
>
> That burst from the seat at our backs. . . .

When the sexual experience is over, the boy, parted from his girl and flushed with success, goes to his motorcycle. Dickey's description reproduces perfectly the happy haste of kinds who got away with it:

> . . . she down Cherrylog Road
> And I to my motorcycle
> Parked like the soul of the junkyard

> Restored, a bicycle fleshed
> With power, and tore off
> Up Highway 106, continually
> Drunk on the wind in my mouth,
> Wringing the handlebar for speed,
> Wild to be wreckage forever.

This poem's greatest accomplishment is in its depiction of youthful passion and resourcefulness, not in its portrait of true love. Doris Holbrook is never as important as an individual woman as she is as the catalyst for the boy's excitement. In this poem we are not confronted with moral sensitivity and complex psychology. Nor is there mystical interaction of the human with the non-human, although Dickey does make some gestures in the direction of pathetic fallacy in order to tie the young lovers symbolically to natural processes:

> So the blacksnake, stiff
> With inaction, curved back
> Into life, and hunted the mouse
>
> With deadly overexcitement . . . .

This is a story of the finding and fulfilling of humanity in natural instincts without regret. These young do not ponder consequences; they act from their energies, and they affirm the wild freedom of having done what was wanted and having freely joined with another human being. There is only a distant fear of reprisal, and that vanishes from the moment "I held her and held her and held her . . . ." The poem is comic partly because the reader believes that this rendezvous might very well take place again, equally without guilt, equally breathlessly, with the young motorcyclist tearing off again, drunk again on the wind.

The repetition of experience implied in "Power and Light" is, from one point of view, tragic. It is a poem about a telephone lineman who feels fully alive only in terms of his work. His wife and children are trouble to him, and at the beginning of the poem he has gone away from them into the basement to drink after work. For most of the poem he is drunk, and he tells how his personal power and light come from his work and his liquor: one satisfies him when he is away from home, and the other lifts him out of the darkness of the basement into the light of his upper house, inured to his unpleasant domestic situation. Insofar as he is trapped by an unchangingly bad home life, the man is tragic; but insofar as he is able to find renewal within himself, and new optimism, he is comic.

This man loves the work of his hands; he is optimistic in turning to physical action for his inspiration, and when that work time is done, he turns inward with drink, to find the "pure fires of the Self." He has comic vitality in seeing the extensions of himself multiplied and spreading world-wide into expression, nothing blocked, everything reaching out and fulfilling the needs of language and emotion:

> . . . all connections
> Even the one
> With my wife, turn good   turn better than good   turn good
> Not quite, but in the deep sway of underground   among the roots
> That bend like branches   all things connect   and stream
> Toward light and speech . . . .

He talks like a ring-tailed roarer, and his courage rises until he cannot simply talk anymore:

> . . . I strap crampons to my shoes
> To climb the basement stairs, sinking my heels in the tree-
> life of the boards. Thorns! Thorns! I am bursting
> Into the kitchen, into the sad way-station
> Of my home, holding a double handful of wires
>
> Spitting like sparklers
> On the Fourth of July . . . .

This kind of going ahead with bluster and stomp makes the lineman one of a long line of comic extroverts: *miles gloriosus*, Falstaff, Pecos Bill, Paul Bunyan, etc. Constance Rourke calls this type the frontiersman, or backwoodsman, but Dickey's interest is not so much in the lineman's word-flinging comic forebears. He sees the man as one who is profoundly conscious of fate and the grave in the midst of his imaginative palaver:

> And I laugh
> Like my own fate watching over me night and day   at home
> Underground   or   flung up on towers walking
> Over mountains   my charged hair standing on end   crossing
> The sickled, slaughtered alleys of timber
> Where the lines loop and crackle on their gallows.
> Far under the grass of my grave, I drink like a man
>
> The night before
> Resurrection Day . . . .

For Dickey, the comic vision is essentially inclusive of all life—people and things, terror and exaltation. One of the differences between Dickey and that other great garrulous includer, Walt Whitman, is that Dickey is more consistent in keeping both the good and evil in mind—unblended, intrinsic—throughout his poetry. The comic vision is a balanced one, enabling men to go on despite deaths and nagging wives, but the deaths and wives are not forgotten. To tramp through the kitchen with Thor's bolts in hand and terrible spikes at heel is not to forget that there is opposition, but it *is* to say to that opposition, ". . . I am a man / Who turns on. I am a man."

Chapter XII

JAMES DICKEY AND THE MOVEMENTS OF IMAGINATION
by George Lensing

The poetry of James Dickey does not belong to a school, a movement, or a method in contemporary American poetry; it is indeed difficult to conceive of a poet writing today who utters more distinctly individual sounds. There are a number of reasons for this: Dickey's willingness to take chances in exploring a wide variety of highly personal experiences; his attempts to convey these experiences by enlarging the boundaries and dimensions of conventional poetic discussion; his deliberate experimentation with metrical forms in seeking out the cadences that best accommodate his personal vision. These are the gropings and trials of any serious poet who is willing to risk occasional failure in order to establish his own authoritative voice. It is hardly a denial of his originality, nevertheless, to suggest that Dickey shares a number of qualities with other post-World War II poets or that he has learned from them.

It is clear, for example, that Dickey's intense subjectivity is part of the new post-modern romanticism that has prevailed in America during the past quarter century. He has also followed many of his contemporaries away from conventional meters, particularly, in Dickey's case, the anapest, toward free verse—though, again, this evolvement has been distinctly personal. Throughout his career as a poet, he has uncovered new ranges of imaginative exploration; it is the nature of this latter quality that deserves special critical attention in the work of James Dickey.

In an essay for the *Southern Review*[1] which appeared in 1967, Ronald Moran and I attempted to define some of the qualities of the Emotive Imagination as we saw them in the work of William Stafford, James Wright, Louis Simpson, and Robert Bly. The article set out to define a new technique recognizable in these poets, where, by a special juxtaposition of images within a poem, the reader is engaged in fitting the parts together to encounter a kind of muted shock of recognition in the end. James Dickey does not write poems according to all the traits of this movement, but he shares with the poets of the Emotive Imagination the same subjective and surrealistic imaginative projections that enable his consciousness to move freely, even phantasmagorically, through disparate activities of reality.

Dickey has himself made a valuable commentary about his use of the imagination in an essay entitled "The Poet Turns on Himself." Here he defines two fundamental elements in his work: his preference for the narrative poem and his desire to fuse subjectivity with objectivity:

> ... I liked poems which had a basis of narrative, that described or depicted an action, that moved through a period of time—usually short—and allowed the reader to bring into play his simple and fundamental interest in "what happens next," a curiosity that only narrative can supply and satisfy. I also discovered that I worked most fruitfully in cases in which there was no clear-cut distinction between what was actually happening and what was happening in the mind of a character in the poem. I meant to try to get a fusion of inner and outer

1. Ronald Moran and George Lensing, "The Emotive Imagination: A New Departure in American Poetry," *Southern Review*, III (Winter, 1967), 51-67.

states, of dream, fantasy and illusion where everything
partakes of the protagonist's mental processes and creates a
single impression.[2]

Dickey's epistemological confrontations with reality do
not include temporal-spatial dimensions in the conventional
sense. "A fusion of inner and outer states" necessarily
includes a pivotal counterpoint between reality and illusion,
between objectivity and subjectivity; a poem's perspective
can reach out in many directions—simultaneously, in anticipation, or retrospectively. Dickey can communicate, for
example, with the past in "Hunting Civil War Relics at
Nimblewill Creek," as well as the future in "The Other": "I
thought of my body to come."[3] The same is true of the
spatial dimension where the poet explores the world from
under in "Pursuit from Under," or from above, as the airline
hostess plunges downward in "Falling."

Dickey's use of the imagination suggests that man's
knowledge of external phenomena is never, in itself, wholly
freed from his native emotional impulses. This is not to
suggest that the reality of the external world is, in any sense,
dependent for its existence upon interior, subjective cogni-
tion; Dickey is no solipsist. However, epistemologically,
Dickey's poems release that which is perhaps most often
consciously repressed in human awareness: the association
and identification of all that is without with varying levels of
interior emotional distortion. The truest reality, the poet
suggests, is empirical reality psychically remade through the
imagination. These creations, however, are not permanent.
While most of Dickey's poems explore various states of
subjective associations and identifications, they invariably

2. James Dickey, "The Poet Turns on Himself," in *Babel to
Byzantium, Poets and Poetry Now* (New York, 1968), p. 287.

3. James Dickey, *Poems 1957-1967* (Middletown, 1967), p. 35.
Unless otherwise indicated, all citations are to this edition.

begin with an objective and undistorted setting of reality, and, what is perhaps more important, the poems almost always conclude with a return to this dimension.

Most of Dickey's poems therefore follow a fairly complex process within the narrative framework: an orientation in the real world of external setting; an entry into a personalized subjective consciousness of that setting; a description by open and free association of the now reconstituted setting through the poet's personal egocentric vision; an ultimate reestablishment of the external setting with the poem's conclusion.

Dickey's penchant for the story-telling narrative necessitates his establishment of a specific setting in place and time with the introduction of each poem. The poet situates himself in the process of doing something—usually active, frequently involving some form of outdoor physical activity. This mode of poetic introduction is important, likewise, for what is to follow. To depart or descend into a personalized world of emotive distortion, it is essential first to erect the boundaries in their undistorted state. The poem will frequently begin, as a result, with an almost journalistic objectivity: "Off Highway 106 / At Cherrylog Road I entered / The '34 Ford without wheels. . . ." (p. 134) or "Down the track of a Philippine Island / We rode to the aircraft in trucks. . . ." (p. 26).

These objective details, however, often contain the germ of what internally is to follow by transformation, metamorphosis, reincarnation, etc. Dickey's desire "to get a fusion of inner and outer states" makes it mandatory that he never totally lose his grasp of the outer state; the poem can never succumb completely to subjectivity. The opening lines of "Hunting Civil War Relics at Nimblewill Creek" illustrate this technique of initial setting:

> As he moves the mine detector
> A few inches over the ground,
> Making it vitally float

> Among the ferns and weeds,
> I come into this war
> Slowly, with my one brother. (p. 98)

The mine detector clearly belongs more to the world of war than to that of a casual day's outing, and, more importantly, the presentation of the "one brother" introduces a crosscurrent of references to the fratricide of civil war and to the poet's relationship with fathers and grandfathers within this setting. The basic symbols of the poem are objectively presented, while their subjective enlargement, though yet latent, is introduced.

A reader is scarcely oriented in the world of a Dickey poem before he is aware that a transformation is occurring. The empirical world of sensory perception is expanded and refocused into an expressionistic world of inner associations. How is this effected? In the largest sense it is done through a process of humanizing various forms of plant and animal life or by revitalizing extinct human life. The title of one poem, "A Dog Sleeping On My Feet," hints at the source of the transference:

> The poem is beginning to move
> Up through my pine-prickling legs
> Out of the night wood,
>
> Taking hold of the pen by my fingers. (p. 55)

In these lines the poet and the poem take on the vitality of the sleeping dog beneath the table. The identification of animal life with human life here originates with the animal; usually, however, that metamorphosis originates within the poet's own consciousness moving outward.

This process of psychic reorientation cannot be totally rational: "Reason fell from my mind at a touch / Of the cords," says the poet in "The Other." (p. 35). It is rather emotive and metaphorical. One is not surprised, therefore, at Dickey's repetitive use of such transferring devices as sleep or dreams to shift the focus of his poem internally ("Near

Darien," "Springer Mountain," "To His Children in Darkness," "The Birthday Dream," "Sled Burial, Dream Ceremony," "A Folk Singer of the Thirties"). The natural blurs
of weather and time provide similar settings for such realign-
ments ("Fog Envelops the Animals," "The Dusk of Horses").
The violence and exhaustion of war, in which Dickey has
been an active participant, function to the same purpose.
("The Performance," "Between Two Prisoners," "The
Driver," "Horses and Prisoners," "Drinking from a Helmet,"
"The Firebombing," "The War Wound," "Victory").

In some cases, it is an unexpected object or gesture on
the part of the poem's protagonist that inaugurates the
change. In "Drinking from a Helmet," for example, the mere
act of drinking water from the headpiece of a dead soldier in
wartime enables the speaker to take on the identity of the
helmet's former owner and, simultaneously, for the poem to
be restructured around the communication between living and
dead: "My last thought changed, and I knew / I inherited one
of the dead" (p. 177). In almost every instance, the vision of
the poet's own consciousness is refocused; the context is
dramatic and the poet acts in solitude and silence.

The entry into the metaphorical and metamorphic
consciousness is accomplished fairly rapidly in a given poem;
the description of that consciousness is what makes up the
essence of Dickey's power as a poet. As Dickey himself has
said, "Strongly mixed emotions are what I usually remember
from the events of my life. Strongly mixed, but giving the
impression of being one emotion, impure and overwhelming—that is the condition I am seeking. . . ."[4] It is indeed a kind of nervousness and intensity that informs the
verse of Dickey. It is only slightly overstating to suggest that,
in his best work, the lines reach out to incorporate the
rhythm and colors of the world itself, dynamically active.
There is none of the bardic tone of the public, orating poet

4. "The Poet Turns on Himself," p. 292.

in his verse; the tone is rather personal because it is psychic, almost psychotic. His poems become a kind of mindscape turning on key images. Even as the poem touches upon an image, leaves it, returns to it, and returns to it again, one perceives that the image is constantly being transformed, enlarged or narrowed. And this transformation is always contingent upon the poet's inner and private self.

The metaphorical identities in a given poem are not precisely delineated; there is nothing of the learnedness of a seventeenth-century Metaphysical conceit, for example. Rather, because of their intense subjectivity, the metaphors are constantly dissolving and reemerging into new forms with a maximum of looseness and elasticity. On a purely rational basis, for example, the reader is doomed to frustration in trying to justify the movement of metaphor in "Fence Wire." Here, the wire of a fence, the meadow, the hawk, the robin, a boy, and finally a man all mesh together into one shared identity.

The virtue of such a technique is that it is always vigorous and never self-consciously precious. At the same time, it can lead to excesses—becoming offensive or even unintentionally comic. "The Sheep Child," a poem about male adolescence and puberty, creates an imaginary offspring of sheep and boy who speaks in the poem:

> *My hoof and my hand clasped each other,*
> *I ate my one meal*
> *Of milk, and died*
> *Staring.* (p. 253)

In "Drinking from a Helmet," the dead soldiers, associated with the young soldier-speaker in the poem who is initiated into manhood, also grow beards:

> To my skinny dog-faced look
> Showed my life's first all-out beard
> Growing wildly, escaping from childhood,
> Like the beards of the dead, all now
> Underfoot beginning to grow. (pp. 173-4)

Such excesses are not frequent, and the risks involved in writing poetry of this nature are deliberately taken on by Dickey. He speaks of his desire to create a poem, not of "neatness," but with "the capacity to involve the reader in it, in all its imperfections and impurities."[5]

It is particularly the association with animal life that one notes as prominent in Dickey's poetry. The protagonist of these poems observes and then shares the identity with animals, recognizing in them the analogues of human personality, frequently of a higher form. In "A Dog Sleeping on my Feet," the poet discovers that his hand has taken on the "language of beasts," and the poem becomes a fox hunt, the poet himself "With the scent of the fox" (p. 56). Or, in "Springer Mountain," the hunter-protagonist, "Deer sleeping," takes on the identity of the deer he has come to kill and moves with him through the forest. The identity with the deer is of course surrealistic and impermanent, but it assumes almost mystical overtones as the poet discovers more fully his own human identity: ". . .what I most am and should be / And can be only once in this life" (p. 132). Another poem, "The Owl King," depicts a blind child, helplessly lost in a forest, and befriended by an owl through whose vision the child is able to see: "I see as the owl king sees, / By going in deeper than darkness" (p. 77).

In all these poems Dickey suggests that the spiritual affinity between man and animals is sacred and that animal life, in its natural beauty and instinctive wisdom, is one to which humans may aspire and in which they may find their own heightened identity. Deer grazing among cattle thus reflect "pins of human light in their eyes" (p. 283), or, in another poem, the speaker, lying in his mountain tent, enters "Into the minds of animals" (p. 109). In every case, it is the associative power of the poet's imagination, poetically

5. *Ibid.*, p. 290.

reconstituted, that establishes such fusions with animal vitality.

Animal life is not the exclusive concern of Dickey's poems, and he shares with the poets of the Emotive Imagination a continuing preoccupation with his own family. "Buckdancer's Choice," the title poem of Dickey's third volume, for which he was awarded the National Book Award, treats of his invalid mother. The father also figures prominently in several poems. It is, however, a brother, dead before the poet's birth, who is a regular inhabiter of Dickey's imagination, and his absorption with that prematurely snuffed out life makes up the subject of various poetic confrontations: "I cannot remember my brother; / Before I was born he went from me / Ablaze with the meaning of typhoid" (p. 82). It is apparently the same brother for whom the poet himself was to be a surrogate, as "The String" explains: "Out of grief, I was myself / Conceived, and brought to life / To replace the incredible child . . ." (p. 21).

Dickey's poetic engagements with the brother occur in various forms; he is seen in the image of his own son in "The String," for example. In "Armor," the poet himself, seeking a "life before life," aspires to assume the brother's identity in some undetermined paradise: "I long to dress deeply at last / In the gold of my waiting brother . . ." (p. 82). "In the Tree House at Night" situates the poet and his living brother first constructing and then sleeping in a tree house. For the poet, however, the other dead brother is also present and it is he who has indeed summoned them to this setting. Lying beside his sleeping brother in the tree house, the poem's speaker attains communication—not by spiritualism or magic—but through the close presence of the living brother, the setting of the tree house, and the power of his own imagination: "The wind changes round, and I stir / Within another's life. Whose life? / Who is dead? Whose presence is living?" (p. 67).

It is noteworthy that in his more recent poetry, the deceased brother has been replaced by Dickey's own living sons in these psychic constructs. In the volume *The Eye-Beaters, Blood, Victory, Madness, Buckhead and Mercy*, for example, the son blowing a wooden whistle communicates with a flock of crows in "The Lord in the Air." In another poem from the same volume, "Messages," the son's talent as a swimmer and interest in the aquatic world prompt the father to commission him "Out of that room and into the real / Wonder and weightless horror / Of water."[6]

The reaching out of the imagination and its fusions with the external world do not always lead to the benevolently serene, and one is perhaps more than ever made aware of the threats to be encountered with Dickey's more recent work. But the recognition of nature's inhospitable capacity was there from the beginning: "We never can really tell / Whether nature condemns us or loves us," he says in the early poem "In the Lupanar at Pompeii" (p. 84). The frantic and violent contortions of the shark, for example, in "The Shark's Parlor," a later poem, are anticipated by the pursuit of the same fish in a poem, "Walking on Water," from Dickey's first volume. The delirium of a dog bitten by a rabid fox is described in "Madness." In the majority of cases, the poet and his imagination seek and find a tranquil meeting ground in nature, but there are other discoveries as well. In "Winter Trout," for example, the shooting of the fish beneath the ice with bow and arrow draws upon the poet a possible verdict of condemnation as he reaches to recover the arrow:

> I froze my right hand to retrieve it
> As a blessing or warning,
> As a sign of the penalties
> For breaking into closed worlds. . . . (p. 128)

The most dramatic example of the predatory forces of nature is witnessed in the poem "Kudzu," where vines and

---

6. James Dickey, *The Eye-Beaters, Blood, Victory, Madness, Buckhead and Mercy* (New York, 1970), p. 12.

reptiles enclose the house of the poem's speaker while he lies sleeping; the kudzu and snakes, through the transformations of the imagination, take on preternatural powers, "Nearly human with purposive rage" (p. 141). The man within experiences the terror of entrapment:

> You open your windows,
>
> With the lightning restored to the sky
> And no leaves rising to bury
>
> You alive inside your frail house,
> And you think, in the opened cold,
> Of the surface of things and its terrors. . . . (p. 141)

Whether the confrontation is with animals, men, or plant life, the poems of Dickey usually involve the humanization of some aspect of non-human life—so that the *persona* of a given poem ultimately discovers something about himself through the act of the imagination. "The Lifeguard" is both typical in technique and use of the imagination and is also one of Dickey's most memorable accomplishments. In his *Self-Interviews*, Dickey has described the origin of the poem:

> This poem does not come out of any situation in which I acted the way the lifeguard does in the poem. I did once help dive for a drowned man in a lake where there was public swimming, and I remember going down ten or twelve feet where everything is blacked out. We didn't have any lights and all we could do was to *grope* around for the body. My fingertips *did* turn into stone, and it *was* awfully cold. There was very little chance that I or anyone else could find the body under those conditions. It's a situation I never want to be in again. I was the father of two young boys in those years and was acutely conscious of the protection motif in the human situation.
>
> The things came together in my mind, and I conceived of the situation in which a lifeguard in a summer camp failed to save a little boy from drowning.[7]

7. James Dickey, *Self-Interviews*, recorded and edited by Barbara and James Reiss (New York, 1970), p. 102.

The poem is structured around the two dominant emotions of guilt and futility on the part of the lifeguard who has a few hours earlier dived in vain for a young drowning boy. The lifeguard, now alone at the site of the drowning, with moonlight playing on the waters, seeks to reenact the earlier scene and, "In quest of the miracle," to bring the drowned boy to life. Stanzas 3, 4, 5, and 6 provide a kind of poetic flashback narrating objectively the events surrounding the drowning and attempted rescue by the lifeguard:

> And my fingertips turned into stone
> From clutching immovable blackness.
> Time after time I leapt upward
> Exploding in breath, and fell back
> From the change in the children's faces
> At my defeat. (p. 51)

In journalistic fashion, these stanzas provide the "real" context of the tragedy to which the anguished lifeguard now subjectively reacts.

The quest of the lifeguard to save the already drowned boy is an act doomed to futility, but, through the psyche of the poem's speaker, a typical confrontation in Dickey's poetry is effected: a communication with the dead. With this objective, the lifeguard returns to the exact spot of the drowning, not by swimming, but by stepping over the waves:

> I rise and go out through the boats.
> I set my broad sole upon silver,
> On the skin of the sky, on the moonlight,
> Stepping outward from earth onto water
> In quest of the miracle. . . .(p. 51)

It is true that a kind of hallucination is occurring and this indeed is the essence of the poem. The human lunacy reproduced upon the lunar reflections on the water is deliberate on Dickey's part. But the poem goes beyond this. The lifeguard, in the actions of his own consciousness, suggests the image of Christ, who also walked on waters, and

was able to resurrect the dead: "I am thinking of how I may
be / The savior of one / Who has already died in my care"
(p. 52).

His desire to save the boy is so powerful that, in his own
consciousness, the lifeguard achieves the impossible
"miracle":

> He rises, dilating to break
> The surface of stone with his forehead.
> He is one I do not remember
> Having ever seen in his life.
> The ground I stand on is trembling
> Upon his smile. (p. 52)

The smile of the drowned boy, imaginatively resurrected, is
the dramatic climax of the poem. This moment represents
the triumph of the imagination in bringing about the
impossible, penetrating beyond ordinary human boundaries—and a like moment occurs as the dramatic center of
most of Dickey's poems. A similar fantasy-enactment, born
also out of guilt and futility, occurs in a more recent poem,
"The Eye-Beaters." Here, the narrator, witnessing blind
children whose hands are tied to prevent their striking their
eyes in angry frustration, instills in them visions of archetypal
animals—exclaiming: "Yes, indeed I know it is not / So I am
trying to make it make something make them make me /
Re-invent the vision of the race."[8]

In this moment of psychic victory over death in "The
Lifeguard" the drowned boy is made to burst, not the surface
of the water to which he is captive, but "The surface of
stone." The water *is* stone and the psychic resurrection
remains elusive and incomplete. The poem concludes with
the final frustration and sense of futility on the part of the
lifeguard: "And hold in my arms a child / Of water, water,
water" (p. 52). These concluding lines from "The Lifeguard"

8. *The Eye-Beaters, Blood, Victory, Madness, Buckhead and Mercy*,
p. 53.

demonstrate a characteristic that is typical in Dickey's poems: the reaffirmation of the external setting, here the water, freed of the distortions of the imagination. This reaffirmation does not deny or reduce the efficacy of the transformation of the imagination; indeed, the speaker of the poem is remade by the experience and is able to reorient himself in the external world with newly acquired benefits as a result of his previous "fusions of inner and outer states." In "Trees and Cattle," for example, the speaker's psychic association with the cattle must be undone, but the return to the independent self uncovers a fuller humanity:

> I go away, in the end.
> In the shade, my bull's horns die
> From my head; in some earthly way
> I have been given my heart. (p. 37)

The association with deer in "Springer Mountain" with whom the poet has shared a psychic identity is impermanent but real; the consequences of that activity, however, will not be impermanent: "A middle-aged, softening man / Grinning and shaking his head / In amazement to last him forever" (p. 132).

The return to the external world is, in some ways, perhaps the most significant progression within the movement of a given poem by Dickey because it implies that the power of the imagination cannot deny the external world permanently. The transformations of the imagination are distortions—even though they are necessary and, at times, mystical. The transformations are given up because the external world of waking consciousness and ordinary social intercourse must finally be restored. The experience of the imagination which takes the *persona* of a given poem beyond the human dimension into various manifestations of plant, animal or extinct human life has, paradoxically, introduced a greater humanity to him and equipped him to accept the restored external world.

This dichotomy between "imagination" and "reality" is

reminiscent of the poetry of Wallace Stevens. Like Dickey, Stevens conceived of inner and outer fusions effected by the imagination; as he states in "The Noble Rider and the Sound of Words," the imagination is "a violence from within that protects us from a violence without."[9] But it is at the conclusion of a Dickey poem that one perceives the fundamental difference between the two poets. Stevens, through a potential and idealized "supreme fiction," aspired to an epistemological poetry that would grant the perceiver the full and permanent transformational power of the imagination while sacrificing nothing of the external flux of reality itself. Dickey acknowledges that the transformational power of the imagination cannot be permanent—even though the antecedent experience has brought the perceiver toward a more fully human self. Stevens desired the distortions of the imagination without the disfigurement of reality; reality must change through the imagination and yet remain the same. Dickey recognizes that the distortions of the imagination must finally yield to the psychically unmutilated phenomena of the external world. The hallucination of the lifeguard in "The Lifeguard" or the "Deer sleeping" of the hunter in "Springer Mountain" may lead to heightened human awareness, but must themselves be finally discarded.

In his most recent work, especially with *Buckdancer's Choice* in 1965 and the poems thereafter, Dickey's imaginative projections have tended to reach out farther toward narrations less formally structured and more psychically exaggerated. It was an almost inevitable direction for Dickey to pursue, particularly as he continued to experiment with freer and more open verse forms. Fewer of these later poems are concerned with human identifications with animal life, for example. In their place one recognizes that the creations of the imagination are straining toward more passionate and

9. Wallace Stevens, "The Noble Rider and the Sound of Words," in *The Necessary Angel* (New York, 1965), p. 36.

even violent subjects–centering upon treatments of sex and death.

"Slave Quarters" is a poem about slavery and the guilt that continues to rest upon the white man generations after the abolition of that institution. The poem is infused with sexual imagery as the *persona* identifies himself with the master whose lust is satisfied upon his slave women:

> I can begin to dance
> Inside my gabardine suit
> As though I had left my silk nightshirt
>
> In the hall of mahogany, and crept
> To slave quarters to live out
> The secret legend of Owners. Ah, stand up,
> Blond loins, another
> Love is possible! (p. 235)

Ralph J. Mills, Jr. has identified this poem and others like it as a "lyricism of the perverse,"[10] though it seems not so much perverse as a kind of *tour do force*. This poem and others like it reveal an unequalled power of poetic showmanship and Dickey seems more lately intent upon dazzling and startling his reader than in the earlier verse. "Falling" is an example of *par excellence* of the new direction in Dickey's work. The poem, inspired by a newspaper account of an airline stewardess accidentally sucked out of an airliner, recreates the act of falling in the consciousness of the girl. In this interlude before death, the stewardess, through the sensation of falling, discovers: "There is time to live / In superhuman health" (p. 294). The poem combines both the technique and the subject of much of Dickey's most recent verse. The highly fluid and open lines, made up of shorter lines within them, containing what Dickey calls the "split line,"[11] are accumulations of successive participial and gerund

10. Ralph J. Mills, Jr., "The Poetry of James Dickey," *TriQuarterly*, No. XI (Winter, 1968), 240.

11. "The Poet Turns on Himself," p. 290.

phrases; the lines correspond to the free sweep of the stewardess' own body. The poem focuses on what is preeminently a moment of acute consciousness, a coming fully to life, for the first time, at the instant prior to death. That consciousness is also epitomized by the girl's sexuality, as her clothing falls from her body and she plunges downward, "desired by every sleeper in his dream" (p. 297).

The poetry of Gerard Manley Hopkins treats of themes radically different from those of Dickey and the tightness and compression of Hopkins' sprung rhythm are hardly akin to Dickey's open-ended looseness. But Dickey might well have been alluding to his own most recent work when he wrote of the nineteenth-century Jesuit poet:

> But the language, the rhythms, the desperate originality of vision, the curious recklessness coupled with the marvelously wrought prosody, the sense of a disciplined outpour that is still, in every syllable, an outpour: these are Hopkins. His world, his work . . . are feverish and a little hysterical. One cannot read too much of Hopkins at a time, for one cannot match his intensity.[12]

Dickey's latest imaginative projections aspire, more than ever, toward a poetry of exhilaration, and this has opened Dickey to new vulnerablities—where form is capable of overpowering content and matter literally becoming manner. There has also been an effort in some of the more recent verse to approximate almost the rhythms of prose—as if eschewing entirely a metrical counterpoint. Poems like "Turning Away" and "Pine" from *The Eye-Beaters, etc.* are blurred by a tendency toward verbosity and overstatement— too discursive to sustain interest.

In looking at the whole of Dickey's poems over the first fifteen years of his career as a poet, one becomes aware that he has staked out a distinct claim in the tradition of

12. James Dickey "The Wreck of the Deutschland," in *Babel to Byzantium, Poets and Poetry Now* (New York, 1968), p. 240.

romanticism. This essay began with the affirmation that Dickey does not belong to a movement or school in modern poetry, and it is difficult to imagine any other contemporary American poet writing a poem like "Falling." Yet, many of the attitudes expressed in his poems are traditional: the belief that many of the most valid analogues for human life are to be found metaphorically in plant or animal life, or that nature offers a refuge from the pressures of society, or that human love, and particularly romantic love, constitutes man's highest faculty, or that emotive and imaginative cognitions can be superior to the ratiocinative. What all these affirmations share is an allegiance to post-Wordsworthian romanticism. When Dickey asserts, for example, in "Reincarnation (II)":

> A word enabling one to fly
> Out the window of office buildings
> Lifts up on wings of its own
> To say itself over and over   sails on
> Under the unowned stars. . . . (pp. 247-8)

he is not only affirming the romantic concept of escape from an urbanized world into nature, but that such an escape can be realized through a "word." It is the word of the soaring bird with whom the man has become identified in the poem, but it is also the word of poetry itself.

Dickey's avowed preference for the "strongly mixed emotions" and the "un-wellmade poem" aligns him with obvious tenets of romanticism. "For the Last Wolverine" is a poem about the disappearing animal who proclaims his identity in "the wildness of poetry" (p. 277) and, later in the poem, seeks to repudiate the "timid poem": "How much the timid poem needs / The mindless explosion of your rage" (p. 278).

Dickey's use of the imagination itself is strongly rooted in romanticism, although it is here that his distinct quality as a poet, his originality, is most affirmed. In his "Ode to a Nightingale," for example, Keats seeks the escape into the world of the bird—both through the "viewless wings of Poesy" and the imminence of death. His own identity, however, is distinct from that of the nightingale: "That I might drink, and leave the world unseen, / And with thee fade away into the forest dim."[13] Dickey pursues the same mode of escape into nature, but his withdrawal is not "with" but "as" the bird: "The make of the eyeball changes / As over your mouth you draw down / A bird's bill made for a man" (p. 81). It is this act of identity with nature in an absolute, though mataphorical, sense that demonstrates the extremity of Dickey's romanticism. It is a point beyond which romanticism cannot go, because, through the emotive fusions of the imagination, the boundaries between man and his environment are erased—temporarily, psychically, metaphorically—but eliminated nonetheless.

The poetry of James Dickey is not social or political, but personal and epistemological. It does not address itself with particular urgency to problems of twentieth-century society, and it seems of limited value to discuss him as a "Southern" poet—in the sense one speaks of Faulkner as a Southern novelist, for example. Dickey has spoken of his need to write poems in order to preserve from oblivion the important experiences of his own life. Poems, therefore, spring from memory and its "incxhaustible fecundity."[14] What Dickey does achieve is the revelation of an intensely personal interior life that is general in confrontation with an external world that is universal. Even more, he seems to suggest that, through the foci of the poems of the imagination, one can discover a constantly new and revitalized world:

> All things that go deep enough
> Into rain and cold
> Take on, before they break down,
> A shining in every part. (p. 157)

13. John Keats, "Ode to a Nightingale," in *Anthology of Romanticism*, ed. by Ernest Bernbaum (New York, 1948), p. 818.

14. "The Poet Turns on Himself," p. 280.

Chapter XIII

James Dickey: Meter and Structure
by Paul Ramsey

"...*the hard and frequently bitter business of discrimination, which is not the wildness but the practicality of hope.*"
James Dickey

James Dickey has an extraordinary lyric gift and has written some excellent short poems which must rank him high among American lyric poets. His best poems open on nature and on spirit. His short poems, however, are better than his long poems and his later long poems are not as good as his earlier ones. In this essay I wish to explain why, by discussing his metrical forms, then discussing the principles of structure in his short poems and showing how those principles apply in his longer poems.

METER: Rising Trimeter

The metrical history of James Dickey can be put briefly and sadly: a great lyric rhythm found him; he varied it, loosened it, then left it, to try an inferior form.

The form of the rhythm is end-stopped rising trimeter, well described by John Hall Wheelock in his introduction to Dickey's poems in *Poets of Today VII* (Charles Scribner's Sons, 1960, pp. 23-24). By "rising" I mean verse in which iambics and anapests predominate.

Why the form has such power can only partly be said. It
is a clearly felt isolatable rhythm which has a base more
insistently felt than that of iambic pentameter, yet capable of
more significant variation than some other strong rhythms,
for instance dipodic or trochaic rhythms. The force can be
apparent in a single verse as in Yvor Winters' remarkable
one-verse poem "Sleep": "O living pine, be still!" Yet the
effect is cumulative also, and shifts of pulsation are felt
within and across verses.

   Theodore Roethke was a master of this form (as of some
others), a poet from whom Dickey admits to having learned
much; but Dickey gains new and strange resonances of his
own. Here is a passage from Roethke's poem "Her Words"
(*The Far Field*, p. 36):

> 'Write all my whispers down,'
> She cries to her true love.
> 'I believe, I believe, in the moon! —
> What weather of heaven is this?'
> 'The storm, the storm of a kiss.'

It is a magnificent lyric tune. Roethke reinforces the basic
pattern by making strong stresses strong and important and
light stresses light and quick, but varies the speed and the
comparative intensity of strong stresses ("Kiss" is nicely
touched, "storm" storms twice.)

   Dickey slows the tune, and darkens it.

> "Sleeping Out at Easter" (first stanza)
>
> All dark is now no more
> The forest is drawing a light.
> All Presences change into trees.
> One eye opens slowly without me.
> My sight is the same as the sun's,
> For this is the grave of the king,
> Where the earth turns, waking a choir.
>
> All dark is now no more.

Dickey's poem moves much slower than Roethke's, is richer
in sound (quantity, timbre, reinforcements), with more stress

on metrically unstressed syllables, and with more parallels of verse shape. The first verse, though straight iambs, is very slow and resonant. Verses 2 and 3 and verses 5 and 6 have the same scansion, iamb anapest anapest (i a a) as does the intervening verse 4 except for its feminine ending. Verses 5 and 6 are parallel in movement word for word.

> My sight is the same as the sun's,
> For this is the grave of the inkg

Verses 4 and 7 have secondary stress, in verse 7 combined with the mid-foot pause ("turns, wak-"). Such verse is incantatory, ominous, rich. Little is said, much gravely hinted, and the power of hinting is in the rhythm, language, imagery, the unitive tone.

Dickey in other poems finds perceptive ways to alter the rhythm, as in the following brilliant passage from "Dover: Believing in Kings" (section 1, last three verses).

> *The king wears newly, at evening.*
> *In a movement you cannot imagine*
> *Of air, the gulls fall, shaken.*

The feminine endings offer new possibilities of counter-working rhythms. The second verse quoted is much lighter and quieter than one expects, and the third achieves a tremulous reversal of movement within the frame: the enjambment from the second verse, the three successive nearly level stresses, the pause have prepared for the shift of motion to the natural trochee of "shaken."

To move much further away from the base is to travel in the mists of a boundary. "Chenille" is a lovely poem (until the narrator intrudes himself in place of the earlier characters and contrives absurdities) which, in its best sections, does vary further, nicely.

> There are two facing peacocks
> Or a ship flapping

On its own white tufted sail
At roadside, near a mill   (section 1)

A middle-aged man's grandmother
Sits in the summer green light
Of leaves, gone toothless
For eating grapes better,
And pulls the animals through   (section 4,
                                          vv. 4-8)

With a darning needle:
Deer, rabbits and birds,
Red whales and unicorns,
Winged elephants, crowned ants   (section 5)

These nice imaginings are rhythmically alive and within hearing distance of rising trimeter. Several verses scan as rising trimeter, namely section 1, verses 3 and 4: 4: 5, 8; 5: 3. Other verses (1.1, 4.1, 4.7, and 5.2) have three distinct accents; two others (4.6 and 5.1) are rising dimeter; hence only 1.2 and 5.4 are really foreign to the basic form, and they are graceful reversals rather than stumbles. These passages represent about the far limit of the varied form; and other passages of the poem go medleyed or flat. One may of course call such passages free verse; but however called the poem is unmistakably influenced by rising trimeter.

To move beyond the form might of course mean to find other oceans and other trees; but Dickey does not, in what I shall call for convenience his middle phase, make many new rhythmical discoveries. The basic form hovers near enough to be felt, sometimes to interfere, but lacks its earlier throbs and dire or delicate changes.

"Cherrylog Road" is an interesting poem in several ways, but rhythmically lax. The trimeter pattern is heard enough so that the poem is not in free verse or prose, but the ground beat is less firm and the variations less significant than in the previous examples. By my count, thirty-six of the one hundred and eight verses do not scan in the pattern. The ones that do not fit are 1.4, 2.2, 4.1, 4.6, 5.3, 5.6, 6.4, 7.1, 7.2,

7.3, 7.5, 8.1, 8.2, 8.5, 9.6, 10.1, 10.2, 10.3, 10.4, 10.5, 11.2, 11.4, 12.1, 12.6, 13.6, 14.2, 14.5, 14.6, 15.4, 15.5, 16.3, 16.4, 17.4, 18.2, 18.3, and 18.5. Of those only eleven have three stresses (2.2, 4.6, 5.3, 5.6, 6.4, 7.2, 7.5, 8.5, 11.2, 14.2, 14.5, 16.3) so that the poem does not classify consistently as 3-stress verse. Counts will vary a little from reader to reader, but the main point is firm: the verse is between rising trimeter and somewhere else, too near the base to escape, too far away to fit. His earlier poetry is, in rhythm, far more powerful; and the poem lacks the intense precisions of the best short-line free verse of H. D. or William Carlos Williams or Robert Creeley.

The earlier rhythms would not simply serve this poem, since they fit the incantatory, and this poem mixes the incantatory and the conversational: in neither element are the meters quite at home. The poem has a clear narrative line, some good (if as usual too much and too careless) detail, and some nostalgias easy to share. But its rhythms do not support its strengths.

Yet the middle phase can work well. "The Scarred Girl" is a better poem in almost every respect than "Cherrylog Road." For once, Dickey keeps to the perspective of another person without intrusion; for once, he praises righteousness. The idea and the detail of the poem are excellent (the "wise" modifying "silver" seems to me the only false note in the poem), and the rhythms quietly hold. If the poem were nearer the base, the gentle dignity would be lost; if it were nearer prose or lax free-verse, its glassy intensity would fade.

"Buckdancer's Choice" is a graceful and attractive poem, though the conclusion is not so grandly nostalgic as it tries to be, and the rhythm has its infelicities. I shall scan the second and third stanzas.

In the invalid's bed; by mother	a a i fem.
Warbling all day to herself	t i a
The thousand variations of one song;	i i i i i
It is called Buckdancer's Choice.	a t i

> For years, they have all been dying   i a i fem.
> Out, the classic buck-and-wing men   t t t t or
>   a i i fem.

The second stanza is delicate and properly gentle; the iambic pentameter with three main stresses is a quiet variation from the pattern rather than an intrusion. But in the third stanza "Buck-" and "Out" grate. The rising rhythm is too strong for the medial trochee "Buckdanc-" not to limp. the "Out" is worse. The unexpected radical enjambment gives the word a thrust it cannot bear. Rhythm, syntax, and meaning collide; one cannot rescue all three.

In the middle phase Dickey often varies the line lengths, two-stress and four-stress verses being the more frequent variants. He also uses 5-stress and 6-stress verses as variants, "Sled Burial, Dream Ceremony" being an impressive example. Here rising trimeter mixes with longer verses, pentameter predominating. The effect is a counterpatterning of trimeter and pentameter, an effect strengthened by the ambiguity of stresses. Actual stress admits many degrees; in scansion a syllable is metrically stressed or not. Hence, unless stress is quite strong or rules govern counting (as they do in accentual-syllabics), one may legitimately count stresses in accentual poetry more than one way. Thus in this poem the verse "The coffin top still is wide open" would scan, in the context of Dickey's earlier verse, as three-stress verse, i a a fem; it can also more calmly scan i i t i fem. Such patterning is hard to sustain but works here, combining plangency and calm. The rhythms fit the quite, somber narrative (Dickey's narrative voice is typically assertive and often blatant) and the great strangeness of tone and detail in the poem.

Dickey's rising trimeter has for its founding mood the darkly incantatory; variation within and from that form can temper, subtilize, weaken, or undo the form's power, as I have tried by these examples to show. When good, it is often very good; I have delighted in many of his poems for years.

METER: subdivided long-line free verse

Dickey has used extensively only one other form, the subdivided long-line free verse which predominates in his more recent work. Long-line free verse is a good form, as is proved by poems by such well-known poets as Walt Whitman, D. H. Lawrence, Robinson Jeffers, and Theodore Roethke, and by a number of other poems including Anne Stanford's "The Riders." It works largely by rhetorical and grammatical parallelism, by sweep, and by accumulation; and its defects ape its virtues: it is open to careless and unheard writing, to facile parallelism and accumulations.

Subdivided long-line free verse raises a logical, hence poetic problem. Long-line and short-line free verse are both valuable forms, but radically distinct. If long-lines are subdivided, then either one has long-line or short-line verse, misprinted; or else some pattern exists in which the unit and sub-unit are consistently meaningful.

That such a two-level pattern is possible is proven by paragraphing. Paragraphs are units, sentences sub-units. The lack of an adequate theory for paragraphing or (after much linguistic effort) for sentences, does not keep good writers from using paragraphs and sentences well. Thus, subdivided long-line free verse, though puzzling to theory, might work well.

Still, writers have made sentences and paragraphs for a long, practiced time. Subdivided long-line free verse is a newer and queerer thing, the burden of proof on its makers and auditors. Unless one can feel a distinct and continued sense of the two levels of division, one is apt to have jerky, overstressed, over-paused prose. Further, one strength of good long-line free verse is the sense of continuity of movement throughout the long line; to lose the sweep is to do away with a major resource of the form.

So much a priori, for what it's worth. My experience of Dickey's verse of this sort leads to the same unhappy conclusion. I may add that I came to such poetry (1) liking much long-line free verse, (2) writing a good deal of it myself, and (3) admiring Dickey's poetry. If I was biased, it was not against the form.

The purpose of the form, in Dickey's own words (in *From Babel to Byzantium*, p. 290) is to give "presentational immediacy," as though experience came in little bursts or chunks or breathless gasps. Experience seldom does. For instance, falling (one of Dickey's poems in this form is called "Falling") is consecutive, although the thoughts of a falling person may be disjointed. A trite metaphor has some validity: consciousness is more like a stream than it is like bursts of breath.

Presentational immediacy is demonstrably an insufficient ideal for poetry, since great poetry gives us experience understood and illumined, not merely mimed or rushed forth. The ideal nonetheless has some real value; the question is whether the form is adequate to that ideal.

Dickey's "The Shark's Parlor" tells a story in the form. The story is told as straight remembered narrative, but is presumably a nightmare or partially sur-natural imaginings; it is told with bloodthirsty gusto. The story has power if many flaws, but the metrical form adds little and detracts much. The long verses have no consistent principle I can infer or intuit. They lack rhetorical and grammatical repetition; they lack long swells and rises; they lack continuity throughout the long verse; they lack any clear sound patterning that finds my ear. The subdivisions are a kind of extremely crude punctuation. The actual variety and phrasing and 'pointing' in poetry or even in speech and good prose, is immense, and any system of rhetorical punctuation or spacing which attempts to show one how to read a passage is grossly inadequate. If one reads "The Shark's Parlor" the way it is spaced, one gets the impression of a hysterical sort of force, but such a reading becomes monotonous very swiftly: it is a bad way to read. Yet, if the spacing does not show how to read, what is it for? I have, in short, found no valid way to read or hear these poems.

"The Fiend" probably uses the technique best: it is a bland, strange, at time sur-natural, off-and-on humorous portrayal of a voyeur. In it the spacings represent natural speech pauses or give valid emphasis. They do little beyond what non-spaced printing would do, but that little helps. Also they probably reinforce the floating dreamlike disconnection of the man's mind, a mood more appropriate here than in some other poems of the kind.

In "The Sheep Child," for me one of the best of Dickey's poems, some interior spacing combines with the rhythms of the middle phase; here the spacing is at least harmless. In "The Birthday Dream," which is essentially a good prose poem, the spacing merely crudens the reading.

In several ambitious poems with internal spacing, the form aims to show different sorts of confusion: in "Coming Back to America" the confusion of a severe hangover (taken very solemnly); in "Reincarnation" the confused states of passing in and out of nature and death; in "Falling" the disconnected thoughts of a stewardess falling to her death; in "A May-Day Sermon" the sexual-hysterical rantings of an insane woman preacher. The best poems in our heritage do not praise confusion, though they admit its existence. These poems praise confusion; the meters compound without intensifying or illumining the confusion. The meters also encourage Dickey's worse faults, including carelessness and prolixity. The great talent remains, but inner power lessens.

METER: some other forms

These two forms, though they predominate, are not all. In particular, the poems in the June 1969 issue of *Poetry* show new departures (which have not been followed up in some more recently published poems). "Blood" is in a charged and driven free verse; "Pine: Taste, Touch and Sight" combines the three-beat line with falling rhythms to create a mood which fits the eating gloom of the passage; and "The Cancer Match," though elaborately placed on the passage, is essentially prose, a lively, dramatic, and highly rhythmical prose; it is a very good prose poem. Prose poetry, poetry in which rhythms work within verses, is a viable and little-used form worth some developing. The rhythms so achieved need not sound like ordinary prose rhythms at all.

Whether Dickey will go farther in any of these three good directions, is yet to see. His abundant talent, energy, and perception deserve better form than they have found in his kind of long-line free verse.

STRUCTURE: The shaping of lyrics

In order to illustrate the principles of his shorter poems, I shall construct a blank verse "sonnet" with concluding rhyme, from one verse from each of fourteen of his poems, altering only punctuation.

> I bear nothing but moonlight upon me
> As I ride blindly home from the sun.
> Coming back, coming back, going over,
> I can stand only where I am standing,
> Unstable, tight-lipped, and amazed.
> I have been given my heart
> Holding onto myself by the hand
> In a gaze from a stone under water,
> Now a lake, now a clamoring chorus
> In a blaze of tears, in that light
> Of the ruined, calm world, in spring.
>
> My blind son stands-up beside me
> For this is the grave of the king.

(Respectively:

> "Into the Stone," st. 5, v. 7
> "Near Darien," st. 8, v. 1

"On the Hill Below the Lighthouse," st. 7, v. 1
"Awaiting the Swimmer," st. 2, v. 5
"Walking on Water," st. 7, v. 4
"Trees and Cattle," st. 6, v. 5
"The Other," st. 1, v. 1
"Poem," st. 11, v. 1 (in *Poets of Today* VII)
"Uncle," st. 1, v. 4 (in *Poets of Today* VII)
"The Performance," st. 7, v. 2
"The Vegetable King," st. 6, v. 4
"The Game," st. 5, v. 1 (in *Poets of Today* VII)
"Sleeping Out at Easter," st. 1, v. 6)

The strange thing is that that "poem" is impressive poetry, and even has one kind of real coherence of development: the narrative of the soul moving in levels and illuminations. The "I" takes a journey in and out of mystery, into and out from a dream kingdom, the kingdoms of death, nature's strangeness, the levels of the soul. He makes discoveries of himself as he travels through different elements (air, water, sun, moon) and comes to feel nearer to other people and to God and nature, his own blind son rising very startlingly beside him as he arrives at the grave of the king.

That one can make a poem with that much coherence and consistency of style from different poems of his, shows how much repetition of theme and image and metrical effect there is in a range of his work. It also shows that such structure is not a fully narrative Aristotelian structure, nor an argumentative structure, nor a movement of inner necessity, organic form, since I clearly worked from the outside in making it. Granting the convention of themes, images, feeling, rhythm, the movement within the general idea of journey, of discovery is quite open. Any move within the tones and themes is possible. That kind of structure is not the only kind he uses in his short poems, but it is important and basic to them. One can illustrate this by looking at a poem of his, "Sleeping Out at Easter," in which the last stanza consists, movingly and credibly, of lines repeated from various places earlier in the poem. Only in his kind of structure could such a thing happen. Anyone who has ever tried to write a sestina or villanelle knows that about all one can do with the forms is to vary themes within some unity of mood. His forms are freer than those restrictive ones, but associative, thematic development is crucial within them. "Sleeping Out at Easter," one of the most beautiful and resonant of his poems, is as near the extreme of that method as any of his poems, though much less extreme than some brilliant poems of Roethke's.

Two other, overlapping methods of his short poems are (1) semi-narrative of an experience, moving back and forth between and among certain objects or beings in the experience, a crisscross method, and (2) direct narrative of an experience, itself literal but conveying various suggested meanings beyond the literal in different ways than normal allegory. The first of these two is exemplified by "Trees and Cattle." A man looks at trees and cattle in sunlight and realizes something of his own nature and the nature of inner and outer reality. Some of the detail is natural ("A cow beneath it lies down"), some metaphorical ("I have been given my heart"), some speculative ("And fire may sweep these fields"), and some sur-natural (" . . . my bull's horns die / From my head . . . "). The shifts between the kinds of language are intricate with the structure. In general the poem happens in one specific place, giving a unity sustained and strengthened by tone, by romantic-religious meaning, and by crisscrossing between the objects and beings in the poem— sun, trees, cattle, I—in a way that feels highly patterned though unpredictable in advance.

Imagine a game played with several posts in a field, the rule being that one may move in any way back and forth between the posts but must touch each post at least twice and must not walk outside of them. Such a game would be less ruled, and consequently less fun, than baseball or—to leave the analogy—than a play by Shakespeare, but it would be much more formal than a game in which one wandered at random in a postless world among land and clouds vanishing into undersea creatures. Dickey's poem works like such posts and clouds, but the posts dominate and the sense of completed design is considerable. The confusion in the poem is contained. A good many of Dickey's shorter poems are like this, many of them using as posts present sensations juxtaposed with certain memories.

"The Driver" is much more straightforward. The narrator, an American soldier on a Pacific island just after World War II, goes joyously swimming. He sees a rusted half-track sunk ten feet under the water, swims down to it, sits in the seat, imagining what it was like to be the driver who he presumed died underwater when the half-track sank. He thinks of life, of death, of pure spirit, stays almost too long, then bursts, frightened, to the surface, seeing the sunlight which goes "for thousands of miles on the water." All works within the narrative frame; the narrative is graceful and persuasive; the analogies are natural rather than forced, the language and the rhythm beautiful. It is a beautiful poem, developed differently from the also excellent lyric "Sleeping Out at Easter." Both techniques are powerful and successful, as can be the crisscross method, which combines them.

These three methods are not the only methods Dickey uses in the short poem, but they are important and central. They all (even "The Driver," since the thoughts of the narrator could be of any length) are indefinitely expansible. They are methods for short poems.

Dickey's problem in the long poem is that those methods are virtually all he has to build with, and are not enough.

"The Owl King" is in my judgment his best longer poem, perhaps because it is the most darkly lyric of them, the most his sort of poem. It is about death and darkness, a world where strangeness is its own being and possession seeks love, but is blind. A blind son dies, goes to live with an owl king, is sought by the father whom he in turn seeks and evades. Three parts are spoken by the father, the owl king, and the son, and the journeyings of spirit are the longings of love. It is a wonderfully strange poem, and the movements to and fro between death, childhood, nature, life, are sufficiently all, so that no more normal shape of narrative is needed. No necessary limit is given to such a poem; it could be two lines or go on endlessly, but the sense achieved of arrived form and length seems powerfully right. This poem is near to the method of "Sleeping Out at Easter," but given more shape by the narrative of search and by the shifts of speakers. Three beings are in important relation, not just the one being who occupies most of Dickey's romantic, egoistic poetry. Even if the three beings are part of a subself, they still create a felt strength of relation often lacking in his work.

"Drinking from a Helmet" is in form like "The Driver" but much expanded. In each poem a soldier takes a helmet off the ground to drink at a water truck in a forward combat zone, leaving his own on for protection. As he drinks he imagines he comes (or does become) one with the spirit of the dead soldier. He finally puts on the other soldier's helmet, has a vision of the other soldier as a boy in California carrying his younger brother on a bicycle. As a consequence of the vision he imagines that he will, after the war, seek out the brother of the dead soldier.

The idea may be sentimental, but I find it appealing, and much of the poem is well done. But the poem is much longer in length, nineteen sections and 169 lines, than it is in substance; and most of it concerns the "I," the dead soldier getting comparatively few lines. Astonishingly the message that the "I" plans to convey to the younger brother is "tell him I was the man," the "I," not the dead brother. What could have been a very good poem is wrecked by expansion of the form, by intrusion of the ego over the meaning (which also accounts for the length—the ideal romantic egoist would find his sensations endlessly interesting), by being—in Roethke's good phrase—"too glib about eternal things," and by inaccurate and absurd detail. The last fault is frequent in

Dickey's work; see the perceptively harsh discussion by Harry Morris in the Spring 1969 issue of *The Sewanee Review*. "The Driver," shorter by over a hundred verses, is the larger poem.

Many of Dickey's situations for poems are brilliant, and many others are skillful. "A Folk Singer of the Thirties" has a powerful and startling protagonist, a mythical figure well invented; a hobo guitarist nailed to the outside of a boxcar by railroad bulls to travel the length and breadth of America for a long time. Taken down by charitable orphans, he preaches to America out of his suffering experience, then at last sells out to TV and to the rich. Such a poem could be any length and stored with any American details. The conclusion (selling out) is only lightly realized, almost an afterthought. The travelling and much of the detail is strongly done and well proportioned. What disappoints is the preaching. The prophet seems to preach power as such: Power of water, oil, whiskey; the rest is vaguely odd but mostly vague. The prophecy, the heart of the poem, is vacant. The poem reminds us how little actually Dickey has to *say*. The poetic theory implicit in his poems and pointed to here and there in his criticism is that poetry should only present experience intensely and immediately, not comment or offer understanding. The theory is false, but even if true, would not help in this instance: a preacher has to say something.

The failure to offer understanding wrecks the conclusion and invades the shaping of "The Firebombing," which is in many ways, despite numerous faults of detail, a powerful poem. The structure is achieved by the crisscross method: the poem juxtaposes memories of bombing Japanese civilians with napalm and the sensations of the pilot in an American suburb twenty years later, with only a little comment. The method of the poem, the switching back and forth, offers some good moments of tenderness, penance, and perceptive irony, but mostly offers a disquieting mixture of confusion and of *celebration* of the intensity of the events. The poem deals with a major issue, the bombing of civilians, but comes to no terms with it. The poem in fact denies the hope of coming to any such terms, ending thus:

"Absolution? Sentence? No matter;
The thing itself is in that."

But guilt and forgiveness, moral understanding and penance, social and individual, do matter, very greatly. The mere assertion of experience does not override them. If the last verse means that experience cannot be judged, or that the intensity of experience is what matters (which would make the bombing good not only for the pilot but for the children burnt to death—being burnt to death is an intense experience), then I profoundly disagree. And I imagine he means something like that, means "The thing itself is the thing itself." But one cannot tell what the last verse means; the reference of the pronoun is too incompetent to yield a meaning. The carelessness is not a mere smudge; it typifies the failure of the method. The poem, pretentiously, has nothing to say.

"Falling" and "A May Day Sermon" are progressively worse examples of his methods. "Falling" recounts the imagined sensations and attitudes of a stewardess (apparently an actual person, the epigraph being a brief quotation from a newspaper account) falling to death from an airliner when an emergency door opened. It does not occur to the poet that the young woman's surviving friends or family (or she herself—Dickey believes in the survival of the spirit after death, his poems often tell us) may properly be offended at her death being used as a vehicle for such imaginings. What she felt and thought we do not know; it is neither likely nor pleasant to think that she played at being sky-diver, bat, hawk, strip teaser aiming at seducing all the farm boys and men in Kansas, on the way to her death.

James McConkey, also deals, in *Crossroads* (E. P. Dalton,

1968, pp. 21-23) with a person falling to death from an airplane. The comparison is instructive; and I would respectfully request the many people who admire Dickey's poem to read McConkey's humane and tender passage thoughtfully.

"May Day Sermon to the Women of Gilmer County, Georgia, by a Woman Preacher Leaving the Baptist Church" has the presumptive excuse that it is narrated by a ranting sexual maniac. Madmen of course can be powerful in literature; one only has to think what William Faulkner or Flannery O'Connor might have made of the narrator's or the protagonist's situation to realize how poorly the poem is developed and performed. The poem consists mostly of a crudely violent mixture of sexual, biblical, and Georgia country detail repeated in various similar hysterical-obscene-blasphemous patches crowded with ridiculous detail, including one-eyed twigs. Among the jumps and screams of the narrator's mouthings, a story is told, told very badly and with pointless obscurity. A farmer finds a used condom in a gully somewhere; he takes that to be sufficient evidence against his daughter, drags her out to a barn and/or a sapling (simultaneously or seriatim matters not), ties her and whips her ferociously while shouting Scripture at her. She screams hatred and defiance at him, boasting of her frenzied lovemaking. She later apparently kills her father with either an icepick or a pine needle in the eye, rides off on a motorcycle with her lover, taking off and throwing on bushes her clothes as they travel (a good acrobatic trick), The lovers ride off the earth, yearly, to a screaming, hysterical, passionate eternity of motorcycle riding, not even apparently ever stopping to make love. The poem applauds evil and (by name) hell. One may hope its absurdities undo its evangelism.

The poem is in plot line a wildly formless retelling of "The Eve of Saint Agnes'." A careful comparison of the two poems, in beauty, intelligibility, structure, quality of imagination and development, moral insight, tenderness, and lovingness should reveal to any thoughtful reader something of the history of romanticism. In serious truth, since there is evil in the world, seeking the greatest intensity of experience is not a sufficient ideal. Dickey has said in *Metaphor as Pure Adventure*, (Library of Congress, 1968, p. 8) that the poet is "absolutely free" to "write" according to laws of . . . / his own devising." Yes, but not free to write well.

More to the present point, a chief reason that this poem is a very bad poem, by a strongly talented poet who has written very good poems, is a failure in understanding the principles by which good or great long poems are possible.

Chapter XIV

NOTES ON JAMES DICKEY'S STYLE
by Laurence Lieberman

In *The Suspect in Poetry*, a first collection of James Dickey's criticism, he eliminates from his canon of taste, one by one, those writers of reputation he finds suspect. Similarly, the development of his art, from book to book, is a conscious stripping away of those techniques of style and mental strategies which have grown suspect after repeated use. In the poems themselves he may leave the explicit record of steps in a willed metamorphosis of style; moreover, each conversion of manner bolsters a corresponding conversion of imagination.

To begin, Dickey's handling of figurative language suggests a basic distrust of the remoteness from human experience of traditional figures of speech. In the early war poem, "The Performance," the speech figures are so closely wedded, annexed, to the human events, it would be a mistake to think of them as being metaphors or figurative-at all, in the usual sense. They are elements of style and expression which are an extension of meaning that is felt to have been already inherent in the experience itself, waiting to be released, or to emerge from the living receptacle as a photo emerges from a negative. The phrases have all the mystery

Reprinted by permission from *The Far Point,* 2 (1968), 57-63.

and suggestiveness of metaphor, but reduce decorative and artificial qualities to a minimum: "blood turned his face inside out," "he toppled his head off," "the head rolled over upon its wide-eyed face," "sun poured up from the sea." Style takes the reader deeply into the experience, intensifying the being in the poem without literary self-consciousness. The poet is telling a story, and if the way he tells the story is as remarkable as the story itself, the *way* of telling remains dutifully subordinate to *what* is told—imparts urgency and intensity to the story.

In the later war poem "Drinking From a Helmet," as in "The Performance," metaphor and personification are so well anchored to harrowing sense impressions that they heighten physical realism:

(1)   I climbed out, tired of waiting
       For my foxhole to turn in the earth
       On its side or its back for a grave.
(2)   In the middle of combat, a graveyard
       Was advancing after the troops . . .
(3)   Where somebody else may have come
       Loose from the steel of his head.
(4)   Keeping the foxhole doubled
       In my body and begging . . .
(5)   I drew water out of the truckside
       As if dreaming the helmet full.

So far are these images from creating the usual remove, the abstracting from literal experience, we expect from figures of speech, these figures seem to carry us into a more intense and immediate literal-ness than literal description could possibly afford. The figures suggest a mind stretching its natural limits of perception to assimilate experience of pain and anguish that can only be apprehended accurately through hallucination. Excruciating mental experience is translated into exact physical correlatives. There is no question of a straining after clever or original images—rather, these queer transpositions of qualities between beings and things are the mind's last resort to keep a hold on its sanity, to stay in touch with its physical environs.

Dickey's use of symbolism is as innovatory as his language. Quite often, the least fully realized poems reveal, in a raw lucidness, ideas and symbols that become the subtly hidden mainstay in the best poems. He draws on the arcane system of thought and symbology in these poems, much as Yeats drew on *A Vision*, in crystallizing the structure of ideas in his most achieved art. We can turn to these poems, as to a skeleton key, for clues that can often be found nowhere else.

Perhaps the first poem of this type is "Dust." In Whitman's vision of reincarnation, traditional worms feed on corpses and bring them back to life through the soil and grassroots. In *Helmets*, Dickey's third volume of poems, his vision is largely confined to that view. However, in "Dust"—a poem in the fourth volume *Buckdancer's Choice*—he moves toward a new vision of reincarnation through worm-like dust motes, "spirochetes boring into the very body of light," a rebirth through sunlight and air. He conceives dust as a middle condition, a mediating form between organic and inorganic matter, life and death, much as scientists conceive the virus as a sort of intermediate limbo—a twilight zone— between plant and animal life. Dust motes seem to embody a partial being, or intelligence, as they wait in air and sunlight for spirits just arisen from the newly dead to whirl through them, changing them into "forms of fire," into "incandescent worms," and finally, amassing them into a shape, "a cone of sunlight." That shape of dust is pervaded by being, and becomes a human. The left-overs, "extra motes," are unable to get into a human form at this time, but ready. They wait.

In "Dust," as in many poems of the later volume *Falling*, Dickey seems to be formulating his symbology into a coherent system of thought, a metaphysics of being. A formal theosophy begins to take shape, if these poems are read conjointly. Subsequently, to trace the development of these symbols in Dickey's cosmos is to find that he has been consistent and scrupulous in carrying them through successive stages of his art. Though particular symbols deepen in meaning and intensity in poems which treat them as primary subjects—"Dust," "The Flash," "Snakebite," "Sun"—their basic identity is consistent with their meanings in other poems. Dickey seems to have deliberately extracted recurring components of his art for specialized treatment, each in a separate poem. Partly, he seems to be trying to find out for the first time why each of these symbols, or symbolic events, has such a powerful hold over his poetic imagination. Also, he is codifying the symbols into a systematized philosophy.

To turn from symbolism to a discussion of the management of line and form, in Dickey's early work the long sentence, often extended over several stanzas, is the chief unit of measure. This type of verse movement served Dickey well for three volumes of work, though in some poems the line falls into artificiality and rhythmic straining when the technique becomes self-imitative, and lacks complete absorption in the subject ("The Island" and "The Scratch").

In "Drinking From a Helmet," Dickey breaks away from the line and stanza units he has grown so attached to. But he stays confined to many of the old sentence rhythms until he begins to evolve the split line of *Buckdancer's Choice*. The form in "Drinking From a Helmet" operates like a film strip. Each frame/stanza focuses on an event, physical or spiritual, separate in time from the others. The movement is that of a film strip, rather than a motion picture, since the pauses or silences between frames are as functional in the poem's rhythmic structure as are the stanzas themselves. This form is an extremely important development for Dickey, since it readily achieves effects exactly opposite to the unbroken flow and rhythmic sweep of most of the previous work. Any such innovation in Dickey's form is accompanied by equivalent modifications in the handling of line and pacing of action.

In the poems of *Buckdancer's Choice* and *Falling*, the

chief unit of measure is the phrase, a breath unit (or breathing unit), as opposed to a grammatical unit. The sentence, as a unit of measure, is all but lost, though occasionally a sentence beginning or ending does seem to punctuate a larger compartment of verse, and more important, a reader usually keeps the illusion that he is moving within the extremeties of a rather free-floating sentence (an illusion that is completely lost, say, in parts of the stream-of-consciousness flow of Joyce and Faulkner). This form adapts perfectly to a welter of experience in flux. The rhetoric keeps drawing more and more live matter into the poem, as from a boundless supply. The entire poem maintains a single unbroken flow of motion. In this respect, the medium owes more to the moving picture, to film technique, than to other poetry. The verse paragraph break is never a true interruption to the rhythmic sweep of the phrase-chain. It merely suggests a shift in perspective, a slowing down and speeding up of the unstoppable momentum, an occasional amplification of the breath-spaces that already separate every phrase from phrase.

Dickey's new form, incorporating the split line, is most successfully managed in the poem "Falling." The triumph of the split line technique in "Falling" is principally the net result of the ingenious variety of effects Dickey is able to achieve by playing off the phrase-unit against the hexameter line unit. The length of the breath-phrases ranges from a single word to a couple of lines. A single line frequently affords as many as five separate phrases:

> Do something with water   fly to it   fall in it
> drink it   rise
> From it   but there is none left upon earth   the clouds have
> drunk it back
> The plants have sucked it down   there are standing
> toward her only
> The common fields of death   she comes back from
> flying to falling

The enjambments between lines are nearly always conscious-

ly functional, whether they interrupt a single breath unit and
break up the phrase, or connect breath units:

>   . . . My God it is good
>   And evil   lying in one after another
>   of all the positions for love
>   Making   dancing   sleeping . . .

The astonishing variety of rhythms is mainly induced by
balancing caesuras within the line, and varying the patterns of
balance in successive lines:

>   She is watching her country lose its evoked master shape
>   watching it lose
>   And gain   get back its houses and people   watching
>   it bring up
>   Its local lights   single homes   lamps on barn roofs
>   if she fell
>   Into the water she might live   like a diver   cleaving
>   perfect   plunge
>   Into another   heavy silver   unbreathable   slowing
>   saving
>   Element: there is water   there is time to perfect
>   all the fine
>   Points of diving . . .

The new form makes available to Dickey avenues of
sensibility and resources of language and subject that were
not accessible in earlier poems. For the poet, what it is
possible to say is mainly a matter of versatility of technique.
In many of the best poems of Dickey's most recent
collection, he is moving toward a more direct engagement
with life-experience than ever before. In "Power and Light"
and "Encounter in the Cage Country," the art is less in the
writing than in the uniquely comic personality of the
persona, who treats his life as a medium for realizing hidden
possibilities for creative existence. There is a strange new
departure here in Dickey's work. The poem hardly seems like
literature. "Encounter" is perhaps the most personally
explicit of all his poems. Usually, Dickey's poems reporting

true personal experience combine explicit concrete reportage with a revelation of meaning, as in "The Hospital Window" and "Cherrylog Road." A reader senses that the poem's discovery is a dimension of the experience that came to the poet as an imagined afterthought, even though the symbolic language and imagery of the poem suggest the experience and the meaning that informs it occurred simultaneously in life. But then, it is the business of poetic art to create that illusion.

"Encounter in the Cage Country" drops the usual barriers between Dickey's life and art. It is as though the writer has reached that stage of his life when the skills of his artistry—comic staging, search for identity, haunting intensification of being—must spill over into his life-experience:

> . . . I knew the stage was set, and I began
> To perform   first saunt'ring   then stalking
> Back and forth like a sentry   faked
> As if to run . . .

Life itself becomes the instrument for creative becoming. It is no longer necessary for the poem to add the dimension of mystery to the experience through consciously willed art, since the personal event itself contains more magic, a sharper ring of truth, than the most subtly imagined poems can afford. The poem creates the illusion, if illusion it is, of being merely a sort of heightened reportage, and it may well stand in the same relation to Dickey's poetic art as *The Sacred Fount* assumes in the canon of Henry James' fictive art. It is a poem that will probably be examined by critics as a key to understanding the fascinating relation between Dickey's art and life. In "Encounter in the Cage Country," Dickey holds up a mirror to himself.

Chapter XV

"His Reason Argues With His Invention"—
James Dickey's SELF-INTERVIEWS and
THE EYE-BEATERS
by Richard J. Calhoun

James Dickey's first novel, *Deliverance*, was such a phenomenal success that anything else he produced in 1970 must by comparison seem rather neglected. Early last year he published his sixth volume of poems, a slim paperback with one of the most ungainly titles in the history of American publishing—*The Eye-Beaters, Blood, Victory, Madness, Buckhead and Mercy*. Then just as the excitement over *Deliverance* was abating, a third 1970 volume, *Self-Interviews*, appeared, simpler in its title but unique in its conception. It seems that Dickey had agreed to expound via the tape recorder on a series of topics outlined for him by two young teachers, Barbara and James Reiss, who feel that they have midwifed something "neither quite like a typical tape-recorded interview nor autobiography" but rather "a new genre, the tape recorded self-interview."

This new genre of the McLuhan era does have a much

1. James Dickey, *Self-Interviews,* recorded and edited by Darlene and James Reiss, New York, Doubleday and Company, 1970.

2. James Dickey, *The Eye-Beaters, Blood, Victory, Madness, Buckhead and Mercy.* New York: Doubleday and Company, 1970.

Reprinted by permission from *The South Carolina Review*, 3 (June, 1971), 9-16.

older literary antecedent which it may not quite equal for literary style or drama, the dialogue in which the writer creates two voices, one his, the other in opposition, in dialectical counterpoint. Dickey has used this form effectively in an essay on Randall Jarrell reprinted in *Babel to Byzantium*. Perhaps this kind of essay reveals more of a duality in Dickey as poet-critic and virile sophisticate than *Self-Interviews*, but with James Dickey as the protagonist the Reisses could hardly fail to produce a volume that is both entertaining and informative.

I would have to say, however, that, no matter how entertaining this spoken Dickeyese may be, the prose is not quite up to the standards of the essays in Dickey's volume of literary criticism, *Babel to Byzantium*, where Dickey's critical judgments are occasionally enlivened by a stylistic barb of true wit. Nothing comes across on the tape recorder to equal the preciseness of his epigram on the poetry of J. V. Cunningham.

> Cunningham is a good, deliberately small and authentic poet, a man with tight lips, a good education and his own agonies. His handsome little book should be read, and above all by future Traditionalists and confessors; he is their man.

The microphone is also not quite conducive to audacious but carefully worded opening paragraphs like that with which Dickey began his essay on William Carlos Williams.

> William Carlos Williams is now, dead, and that fact shakes one. Has any other poet in American history been so actually useful, usable, and influential? How many beginning writers took Williams as their model, were encouraged to write because . . . Well, if that is poetry, I believe I might be able to write it too!

The only comparable passage that filters through the tape recorder to the pages of *Self-Interviews* is Dickey's account of a poem written in an advertising office and typed by a new secretary.

I wrote this poem "The Heaven of Animals" in an advertising office. I had a new secretary and I asked her to type it for me. She typed up the poem letter-perfect and brought it to me. Then she asked, "What is it? What company does it go to?"
"This is a poem," I said.
"It is?"
"Yes, it is, I hope."
"What are we going to sell with it?" she asked.
"God," I said, "We're going to sell God."
"Does this go to a religious magazine or something?"
"No, I'm going to publish it in *The New Yorker*," I told her.
And, as it happened, that's where it came out.

If *Self-Interviews* seldom equals the wit of Dickey's best critical prose, it has the true sound of Dickey speaking, a marvel in itself as anyone who has heard him read will testify; and it is a handbook of information about Dickey and his poems, compiled not by some assistant professor at a midwestern university but by the poet himself. Part one, "The Poet at Mid-Career," provides details about Dickey's creative psyche from the first awakenings of his interests in poetry through the publication of *Poems 1957-1967*. Part two, "The Poem as Something That Matters," consists of five sections, one each on Dickey's first five volumes of poetry. Dickey's critical pretensions are very modest. He makes it clear that he is not trying "to impose an official interpretation on the poems" or "to preclude anybody else's interpretation. . . . I have been asked on this occasion, though, what my poems are supposed to be about from my standpoint and what I have tried to do in them."

What *is* surprising is that Dickey's comments are not too surprising. Very little transpires which would show that his explicators have ever been dead wrong. Instead, in part one we have further evidence for what his critics have assumed all along. Dickey has "never been able to dissociate the poem from the poet." He doesn't "believe in Eliot's theory of autotelic art." He feels that the value of literature "must be maintained if we're going to have any humanity left at all."

He regards a poem as "that kind of personal connection of very disparate elements under the fusing heat of the poem's necessity." He just doesn't "have beautiful Mozartian flights of the imagination." He is not surprisingly "much more interested in a man's relationship to the God-made world, or the universe-made world, than to the man-made world." He is drawn "to a philosopher like Heraclitus" and has as "personal heroes of the sensibility John Keats, James Agee, and Malcolm Lowry." The last two items may be news.

Part two is of greater use to students of Dickey's poems. It is informative and useful and often good reading, even if Dickey fails to evoke any sense of a critical recreation of the creative process as Stephen Spender did in "The Making of a Poem" and Allen Tate did in his essay on his own "Ode to the Confederate Dead."

Some reviewers have complained that Dickey reveals himself very cautiously, giving his reader "a routine milking of the glands" rather than the "total act of the body" that he feels meaningful communication should involve. I would not call *Self-Interviews* or anything that James Dickey's imagination produces routine, but the reader may well feel that the Dickey he encounters here is the public Dickey speaking on the level of good conversation and that the voice of the inner man is not heard.

The passage in *Self-Interviews* that best provides a lead for a description of *The Eye-Beaters, Blood, Victory, Madness, Buckhead and Mercy* is Dickey's comment on his poem "The Lifeguard" from his early volume, *Drowning With Others.*

> Allen Tate once said that he thought of his poems as commentaries on those human situations from which there was no escape. "The Lifeguard" is my idea of a poem about one of those human situations from which there is no escape.

There are seventeen poems in *The Eye-Beaters.* An even dozen are concerned with situations from which there is no escape—aging, illness, and death; and it is these poems which have attracted the attention of the reviewers. This part of Dickey's book seems to be his "no exit," that is, (if Dickey will pardon the trite phrase) his most existential volume.

Dickey has indicated in a recent interview that he is pleased with *The Eye-Beaters*, regarding it as perhaps his most successful single volume. His reviewers have not been exactly unanimous in thier agreement with Dickey's judgment. Some have objected to it on thematic grounds, feeling that Dickey at his best is a poetic celebrant of the life force and that he cannot handle darker themes as successfully. Other critics have found a falling off in style. Dickey, the poet of "open forms," has not quite successfully mated the freedom of his split line with the discipline of more nearly regular stanzaic forms, *etc.* Critics always seem to voice a feeling of having been betrayed when poets change a successful style or theme.

There is some truth to these charges, however, and I must agree partially with the complaints about Dickey's style. Dickey is a bit too often both rhetorical and commonplace. I do not detect the note of hysteria that the ears of some critics have caught, but I was bothered by an overuse of rhetorical devices which tend to make Dickey sound somewhat melodramatic. Several of Dickey's poems in this volume bear a heavy freight of interjections ("Ah, it was then, Chris," *etc.*) and apostrophes ("O son," "O Chris," "O parents," "O justice scales") as well as rhetorical questions. Occasionally—and only occasionally—Dickey sounds like Randall Jarrell, who was a bit too fond of such devices.

In fact, it seems that stylistically Dickey is heading in two opposite directions in this volume. In a poem like "The Eye-Beaters" he seems to be moving impressively ahead, even beyond the "big forms" of his earlier poems, toward archetypal images; whereas in other poems he seems to revert to the direct statements of his early poems and to come up with something too commonplace.

> . . . Not bad! I always knew it would have to be
>   somewhere around
> The house . . .
>
> ("Diabetes, I")
>
> . . . I'm going in Tyree's toilet
> and pull down my pants and take a shit.
>
> ("Looking for the Buckhead Boys")

When he touches on his illnesses, real and imaginary, his style suggests that of Robert Lowell in *Life Studies* rather than the expansive imagination of James Dickey evident in his previous volumes.

> My eyes are green as lettuce with my diet,
> My weight is down . . . .
>
> ("Under Buzzards")

But in spite of such tatters in his poetic garments James Dickey is still a very fine poet, and his most recent volume of poetry does not represent as abrupt a change in his style or thematics as some of his reviewers have assumed or as my few examples might have suggested. A central concern of Dickey's poetry has always been contact with the other, represented variously as animalistic natural forces, the dead, Being itself.

In his first volume, *Into the Stone,* death is regarded as a change of being, not a thing to be feared; and the dead are accessible through the imagination. An exchange of being with the dead is a part of Dickey's obsession to understand through an act of faith in his imagination events which reason alone cannot comprehend. In *Drowning with Others* this "way of exchange" is a chief preoccupation of Dickey's, but here he seems for the first time reluctant to commune with the dead, and the exchange is predominantly with vital animal forces. In his next volume, *Helmets,* even the communion with the Other has become suspect as something only temporary and even potentially dangerous, since the *persona* may lose power as well as gain it. In *Buckdancer's*

Choice there are, for the first time, unsuccessful attempts at communion. In one of the finest poems in the volume, "The Firebombing," Dickey tries to transpose himself from his airplane down to the destruction he is creating below. This time, however, his imagination is incapable of penetrating such barriers as the aesthetic distance created by the space barrier, the beauty of the flight, and peacetime, middle-class comfort.

In the "Falling" section of *Poems 1957-1967* there is a further stage in Dickey's movement away from a concern with vital forces to the threat of destructive forces. Here he becomes concerned with the problem of how to face death and other threats to vitality and with the resources and rituals the merely human being has to draw on in such encounters. In the title poem "Falling," an airline hostess falling to her death realizes under the extreme pressures of her contracted life-span that the only possibility of transcendence lies in making her death a mystery for the farm boys below. Consequently, she affirms her life at the very moment of her death, stripping herself naked and preparing her body for the last fatal and sacrificial reunion with the fertile earth. She discovers within herself a resource which permits transcendence.

In another poem, "Power and Light," there is a suggestion that the pole climber represents a new concept that Dickey has of the poet, in that he is able to find the sources of his power—his ability to make connections for "the ghostly mouths" carried over the lines—*underground*, in the silent dark of his basement. Dickey seems to suggest that the "secret" of existence that he has been pursuing comes from a confrontation not with the natural world but with the "dark" of one's own death. A key passage in the poem seems to look back toward his earliest personal poems and ahead to new directions.

>   . . . Years in the family dark have made me good

> At this   nothing else is so good   pure fires of the Self
> Rise crooning in lively blackness....

In *Self-Interviews* Dickey provides further evidence of continuity by confirming what his reviewers have always known, that there is a connection between the chronology of his poems and that of his life. In *The Eye-Beaters* the reader encounters a person who is aware that his own youth is gone, that his life-space, like that of the air hostess in "Falling," has narrowed. "Two Poems of Going Home" invokes rather effectively the inmost secret fears of a middle-aged man who finds only memories left at the locale of his youth.

> ... Why does the Keeper go blind
> With sunset? The mad, weeping Keeper who can't keep
> A God-damned thing   who knows he can't keep everything
> Or anything alive: none of his rooms, his people
> His past, his youth, himself,
> But cannot let them die? ...
> ("Living There")

"The Cancer Match" uses that prerogative of the poet that Dickey describes in *Self-Interviews* of lying convincingly and projects a fatal illness.

> I see now the delights
>
> Of being let "come home"
> From the hospital.
> Night!
> I don't have all the time
> In the world, but I have all night.
> I have space for me and my house,
> And I have cancer and whiskey
> In a lovely relation

In *Self-Interviews* Dickey describes his celebration of life forces in his earlier poems as the reaction of a survivor of two very destructive wars. Rather than hysteria, the emotions that make themselves known to the reader in the poems of

The Eye-Beaters are gratitude at having survived so far the destructive forces of nature and praise of the courage to take risks as a means of coping with the fear of death.

In the poem "The Eye-Beaters" Dickey implies the new poetics of the present volume. The poet must describe encounters with the most basic life experiences, including destructive as well as life-giving forces. He must see the image of the blind children as archetypal and imagine the reason for the children beating their eyes.

> Therapists, I admit it, it helps me to think
> That they can give themselves, like God from their scabby fists,
> the original
>
> Images of mankind: . . .

In *The Eye-Beaters*, consequently, Dickey presents situations, real and imaginary, where his *persona* is faced with the fear of death. He must imagine ways to cope with this fear. One solution, already indicated, is to take risks. In "Giving a Son to the Sea," the father urges his son to take to the sea to affirm life even though the sea may swallow him up. In "Under Buzzards," the diabetic drinks the beer that could kill him.

At any rate, Dickey makes it clear that the reality of death must be confronted. In "Looking Up the Buckhead Boys," the poet feels the compulsion to look into his school yearbook of more than thirty years before—"The Book of the Dead"—and to go out to face what has happened to the "Buckhead Boys." Like some of his reviewers, I regret the loss of those powerful notes of Dickey's celebration of life; every poet today must have his existential volume, and, for better or worse, this is Dickey's. Here he seems to be attempting to say that a confrontation with death and its associated destructive forces (aging, disease, violence, and madness) may lead to fear but it may also lead to a realization of and an appreciation of the value of life. It should be noted that the volume includes a unique and almost semi-official celebration of the courage to take risks.

Dickey reprints opposite a black, blank page the two poems from *Life Magazine* in honor of the Apollo astronauts who first walked on the dead surfaces of the moon and, from that perspective, appreciated in the black sky of the universe the blue life-light of their own planet.

> . . . To complete the curve   to come back
> Singing with procedure   back through the last dark
> Of the moon, past the dim ritual
> Random stones of oblivion, and through the blinding edge
> Of moonlight into the sun
>
> And behold
>
> The blue planet steeped in its dream
>
> Of reality, its calculated vision shaking with
> The only love

JAMES DICKEY: A CHECKLIST

This checklist is intended as a supplement to Eileen K. Glancy's "James Dickey: A Bibliography," *Twentieth Century Literature,* XV (April 1969), 45-61. It includes those items that were omitted or listed erroneously, as well as those that have appeared since April 1969.

Robert W. Hill
University of Illinois
Urbana, Illinois

BOOKS AND PAMPHLETS BY DICKEY

"Into the Stone," in *Poets of Today VII*, ed. John Hall Wheelock. New York, 1960.

"The Death and Keys of the Censor," *Sewanee Review*, LXIX (Spring 1961), 318-32.

"Randall Jarrell," in *Randall Jarrell 1914-1965*, eds. Robert Lowell, Peter Taylor, Robert Penn Warren, pp. 33-48. New York, 1967.

Drowning with Others. Middletown, Connecticut, 1962.

Two Poems of the Air. Portland, Oregon, 1964.

Helmets. Middletown, Connecticut, 1964.

The Suspect in Poetry. Madison, Minnesota, 1964.

Buckdancer's Choice. Middletown, Connecticut, 1965.

"Barnstorming for Poetry," *New York Times Book Review*, January 3, 1965, pp. 1, 22-23.

"James Dickey on Poetry and Teaching," *Publishers' Weekly*, March 28, 1966, p. 34.

Poems 1957-1967. Middletown, Connecticut, 1967.

The Poems of James Dickey (1957-1967) [Recording], directed by Authur Luce Klein. Spoken Arts (SA 984) [LC No. R67-39521]. New Rochelle, N.Y.: Spoken Arts, Inc., 1967.

"Spinning the Crystal Ball: Some Guesses at the Future of American Poetry." Library of Congress, 1967.

"The Son, the Cave, and the Burning Bush," introduction to *The Young American Poets,* ed. Paul Carroll. Chicago, 1968.

Babel to Byzantium: Poets and Poetry Now. New York, 1968.

"Metaphor as Pure Adventure: A Lecture Delivered at the Library of Congress, December 4, 1967." Library of Congress, 1968.

"Comments to Accompany *Poems 1957-1967,*" *Barat Review* (Barat College), III (1968), 9-15.

"A Poet Witnesses a Bold Mission," *Life,* November 1, 1968, p. 26.

Deliverance. Boston, 1970.

The Eye-Beaters, Blood, Victory, Madness, Buckhead and Mercy. Garden City, New York, 1970.

Self-Interviews. New York, 1970.

"Two Days in September" [Excerpts from *Deliverance*], *Atlantic Monthly,* February 1970, pp. 78-108.

"P.P.A. Authors' Press Conference" [Excerpts], *Publishers' Weekly,* March 23, 1970, pp. 27-29.

"The Process of Writing a Novel," *The Writer,* June 1970, pp. 12-13.

"Poet Tries to Make a Kind of Order" [Excerpts from *Self-Interviews,* eds. J. and B. Reiss], *Mademoiselle,* September 1970, pp. 142-43.

Exchanges. Bloomfield Hills, Michigan: Bruccoli-Clark, 1971.

Sorties: Journal and New Essays. New York, 1971.

POEMS NOT IN *POEMS 1957-1967* OR *THE EYE-BEATERS*

"By Canoe Through the Fir Forest," *New Yorker,* June 16, 1962, p. 32. [Found in *Poems* as a section of "On the Coosawattee."]

"Camden Town," *Virginia Quarterly Review,* XLVI (Spring 1970), 242-43.

"The Courtship," *Mutiny,* No. 12 (1963), 97-98.

"Drums Where I Live," *New Yorker,* November 29, 1969, p. 56.

"Exchanges," *Atlantic Monthly,* September 1970, pp. 63-67.

"False Youth: Autumn: Clothes of the Age," *Atlantic Monthly,* November 1971, p. 67.

"For the Death of Vince Lombardi," *Esquire,* September 1971, pp. 142-43.

"The Gamecocks," *Poetry,* January 1962, pp. 240-42.

"Haunting the Maneuvers," *Harper's,* January 1970, p. 95.

"Mindoro, 1944," *Paris Review,* No. 22 (Autumn/Winter 1959-1960), 122-23.

"The Moon Ground," *Life,* July 4, 1969, p. 16C.

"Orpheus Before Hades," *New Yorker,* December 5, 1959, p. 52.

"Paestum," *Shenandoah,* XIV (Winter 1963), 7-10.

"Rain Guitar," *New Yorker,* January 8, 1970, p. 36.

"Root-Light, or the Lawyer's Daughter," *New Yorker,* November 8, 1969, p. 52.

"The Swimmer," *Partisan Review,* XXIV (Spring 1957), 244-46.

"The Twin Falls," *Choice,* I (Spring 1961), 50-51.

"Walking the Fire Line," *Mutiny,* No. 12 (1963), 96-97.

PROSE ARTICLES BY DICKEY

"Barnstorming for Poetry," *New York Times Book Review*, January 3, 1965, pp. 1, 22-23.

"The Death and Keys of the Censor," *Sewanee Review*, LXIX (Spring 1961), 318-32.

"James Dickey on Poetry and Teaching," *Publishers' Weekly*, March 28, 1966, p. 34.

"A Poet Witnesses a Bold Mission," *Life*, LXV (November 1, 1968), 26.

"The Process of Writing a Novel," *The Writer*, LXXXIII (June 1970), 12-13.

"Randall Jarrell," in Robert Lowell, Peter Taylor, Robert Penn Warren, eds. *Randall Jarrell 1914-1965*. New York 1961. pp. 33-48.

"The Son, the Cave, and the Burning Bush," introduction to *The Young American Poets*, ed. Paul Carroll. Chicago, 1968.

REVIEWS OF *BABEL TO BYZANTIUM*

Adams, Phoebe. "Potpourri," *Atlantic Monthly*, CCXXI (May 1968), 114.

American Literature, XL (November 1968), 436.

Booklist, LXV (September 1, 1968), 32.

Calhoun, Richard J. "Whatever Happened to the Poet-Critic?" *Southern Literary Journal*, I (Autumn 1968), 75-88.

Choice, V (October 1968), 950.

Cushman, Jerome. *Library Journal*, XCIII (April 1, 1968), 1485.

Fuller, E. *Wall Street Journal*, August 15, 1968, p. 10.

Kirkus Service, XXXVI (March 1, 1968), 300.

Lask Thomas. "Books of the Times: Writer Turned Reader," *New York Times*, May 10, 1968, p. 45.

Lieberman, Laurence. "Poet-Critics and Scholar-Critics," *Poetry*, CXV (February 1970), 346-352.

Maloff, Saul. "Poet Takes His Turn as Critic," *Book World*, June 30, 1968, Sec. 9, p. 10.

Packard, W. *Spirit*, November 1968, p. 150.

Pritchard, William H. "Why Read Criticism?" *Hudson Review*, XXI (Autumn 1968), 585-92.

Publishers' Weekly, April 1, 1968, p. 35.

Stepanchev, Stephen. *New Leader*, LI (May 20, 1968), 33.

Virginia Quarterly Review, XLIV (Autumn 1968), cliii.

REVIEWS OF *BUCKDANCER'S CHOICE*

Booklist, LXII (December 1, 1965), 350-51.

"Down from the Mountain," *Times Literary Supplement*, January 27, 1966, p. 65.

Hochman, Sandra. "Some of America's Most Natural Resources," *Book Week*, February 20, 1966, pp. 4, 11.

Huff, Robert. "The Lamb, the Clocks, the Blue Light," *Poetry*, CIX (October 1966), 44-48.

Monaghan, Charles. *Commonweal*, LXXXIV (April 15, 1966), 120-22.

Robinson, J. K. "Terror Lumped and Split: Contemporary British and American Poets," *Southern Review*, New Series, VI (Winter 1970), 216-28.

Strange, William. "To Dream, to Remember: James Dickey's *Buckdancer's Choice*," *Northwest Review*, VII (Fall/Winter 1965-66), 33-42.

REVIEWS OF *DELIVERANCE*

Algren, Nelson. "Tricky Dickey," *Critic*, XXVIII (May/June 1970), 77-79.

Avant, John Alfred. *Library Journal*, XCV (March 1, 1970), 912.

Bedient, Calvin. "Gold-Glowing Mote," *Nation*, CCX (April 6, 1970), 407-08.

Clemons, Walter. "James Dickey, Novelist," *New York Times Book Review*, March 22, 1970, p. 22.

Connell, Evan S., Jr. "Review: *Deliverance,* by James Dickey," *New York Times Book Review,* March 22, 1970, pp. 1, 23.

"Everyone's Notion of a Poet," *Time,* XCV (April 20, 1970), 92.

"James Dickey Tells About *Deliverance,*" *The Literary Guild Magazine,* April 1970, pp. 6-7.

"Journey Into Self," *Time,* XCV (April 20, 1970), 92-93.

Keller, Marcia. *Library Journal,* XCV (May 15, 1970), 1969.

Lehmann-Haupt, C. "Men in Groups," *New York Times,* March 27, 1970, p. 31.

Mahon, D. *The Listener* (London), Sept. 10, 1970, p. 352.

Marsh, Pamela. *Christian Science Monitor,* April 2, 1970, p. 7.

Raymont, Henry. "3 Book Clubs Pick Paul Horgan Novel," *New York Times,* July 31, 1970, p. 12.

Ricks, Christopher. "Man Hunt," *New York Review of Books,* April 23, 1970, pp. 37-41.

Rosenthal, Lucy. "A Novel of Man, the Forest, Death and Heroism," *Book World,* March 15, 1970, pp. 1, 3.

Samuels, Charles Thomas. "What Hath Dickey Delivered?" *New Republic,* April 18, 1970, pp. 23-26.

Schlueter, P. *Christian Century,* June 17, 1970, p. 765.

Sissman, L. E. "Poet Into Novelist," *New Yorker,* XLVI (May 2, 1970), 123-26.

Stone, Robert. "Adrift in Our Ancestral Jungle," *Life,* LXVIII (March 27, 1970), 10.

Thwaite, A. "Out of Bondage," *New Statesman* (London), Sept. 11, 1970, pp. 310-11.

Times Literary Supplement, Sept. 11, 1970, p. 989.

Wolf, Gregory. *Best Sellers,* XXX (April 1, 1970), 11-12.

Wolff, Geoffrey. "Hunting in Hell," *Newsweek,* LXXV (March 30, 1970), 95A,96.

Yoder, Ed. *Harper's,* CCXL (April 1970), 106-07.

REVIEWS OF *HELMETS*

Galler, David. "Versions of Accident," *Kenyon Review*, XXVI (Summer 1964), 581-84.

Ricks, Christopher. "Spotting Syllabics," *New Statesman*, LXVII (May 1, 1964), 684-85.

Woods, John. "Five Poets," *Shenandoah*, XVI (Spring 1965), 85-91.

REVIEWS OF *THE EYE-BEATERS, BLOOD, VICTORY, MADNESS, BUCKHEAD AND MERCY*

Adams, Phoebe. *Atlantic Monthly*, CCXXV (March 1970), 146.

Avant, J. A. *Library Journal*, XCV (March 1970), 902-903.

Booklist, LXVI (June 15, 1970), 1251.

Howard, Richard. "Resurrection for a Little While," *Nation*, CCX (March 23, 1970), 341-42.

Klevs, William. [Letter on "Looking for the Buckhead Boys"], *Atlantic Monthly*, February 1970, p. 49.

Leibowitz, Herbert. "The Moiling of Secret Forces," *New York Times Book Review*, Nov. 8, 1970, VII, pp. 20, 22.

Robertson, William K. [Letter on "Looking for the Buckhead Boys"], *Atlantic Monthly*, February 1970, p. 49.

REVIEWS OF "INTO THE STONE"

Evans, Oliver. "University Influence on Poetry," *Prairie Schooner*, XXXV (Summer 1961), 179-180.

REVIEWS OF *POEMS 1957-1967*

Booklist, LXIII (June 1, 1967), 1027.

Dodsworth, M. *Listener*, LXXIX (June 25, 1968), 842.

Hill, Robert W. "Sacramental Verse," *South Atlantic Bulletin*, XXXII (November 1967), 27.

Katz, Bill. *Library Journal*, XCII (April 1, 1967), 1497.

Kirkus Service, XXXV (February 15, 1967), 236.

"Leaps and Plunges," *Times Literary Supplement*, May 18, 1967, p. 420.

Lieberman, Laurence. "The Expansional Poet: A Return to Personality," *Yale Review*, LVII (Winter 1968), 258-71.

———. "The Worldly Mystic," *Hudson Review*, XX (Autumn 1967), 513-20.

Meredith, William. "A Good Time for All," *New York Times Book Review*, April 23, 1967, pp. 4, 46.

Publishers' Weekly, February 20, 1967, p. 142.

Stafford, William. "Supporting a Reputation," *Books Today*, May 14, 1967, p. 9.

Symons, Julian. "Moveable Feet," *New Statesman*, LXXI (June 16, 1967), 849.

REVIEWS OF *SELF-INTERVIEWS*

Maddocks, Melvin, "The Poet Speaks," *Christian Science Monitor*, Nov. 12, 1970, p. 8B.

Nuren, Dorothy. "Transcriptions of Interviews with Dickey," *Library Journal*, XCV (Sept. 15, 1970), 2926.

Wimsatt, Margaret. "Self-Interviews," *Commonweal*, Feb. 19, 1971, pp. 501-503.

Yardley, Jonathan. "More of Superpoet," *New Republic*, CLXIII (Dec. 5, 1970), 26-27.

REVIEWS OF *SORTIES: JOURNAL AND NEW ESSAYS*

Booklist, LXVIII (Jan. 15, 1972), 411.

Broyard, Anatole. "Dickey's Likes and Dislikes," *New York Times*, Dec. 17, 1971, p. 37.

Kalstone, David. *New York Times*, Jan. 23, 1972, VII, pp. 6, 24.

REVIEWS OF THE *SUSPECT IN POETRY*

Howes, Victor. "Genius and Bogus," *Christian Science Monitor*, December 3, 1964, p. 8B.

Kostelanetz, Richard. "Flyswatter and Gadfly," *Shenandoah*, XVI (Spring 1965), 92-95.

"Bookmarks," *Prairie Schooner*, XXXIX (Summer 1965), 175.

"Some Recent Books," *Carleton Miscellany*, VI (Winter 1965), 122-26.

Williams, Hugo. *London Magazine*, October 1965, p. 101.

REVIEWS OF *TWO POEMS OF THE AIR*

Duncan, Robert. "Oriented by Instinct, By Stars," *Poetry*, CV (November 1964), 131-33.

Scarbrough, George. "One Flew East, One Flew West, One Flew Over the Cuckoo's Nest," *Sewanee Review*, LXXIII (Winter 1965), 137-50.

GENERAL

"Book Awards Go to 4 U.S. Writers," *New York Times*, March 16, 1966, p. 42.

Burns, G. *Southwest Review*, LIII (Summer 1968), 332-33.

Calhoun, Richard J. *James Dickey* (I & II). Cassette Tapes Nos. 175, 176, Deland, Florida: Everett/Edwards Press, 1971.

Carroll, Paul. "The Smell of Blood in Paradise," in *The Poem in Its Skin*. Chicago and New York, 1968. pp. 43-49.

Clark, Robert. "James Dickey: American Poet," *Australian Book Review*, March 1968, p. 83.

DeMott, Benjamin. "The 'More Life' School and James Dickey," *Saturday Review*, LIII (March 28, 1970), 25-26, 38.

Esty, Jane, and Paul Lett. "A Mutiny Alert," *Mutiny*, IV (Winter 1961/62), 3-9.

"Everyone's Notion of a Poet," *Time*, XCV (April 20, 1970), 92.

"Four Authors Are Given National Book Awards," *Publishers' Weekly*, March 21, 1966, pp. 47-48.

Glancy, Eileen. *James Dickey: The Critic as Poet*. Annotated Bibliography. Troy, New York: Whitston Publishing Co., 1971.

Hollander, John, ed. *Poems of Our Moment*. New York, 1968.

Howard, Richard. "James Dickey," in *Alone with America*. New York, 1969. pp. 75-98.

———. "On James Dickey," *Partisan Review*, XXXIII (Summer 1966), 414-28, 479-86.

Lieberman, Laurence. "Notes on James Dickey's Style," *The Far Point*, No. 2 (Spring/Summer 1969), 57-63.

Martz, William J., ed. *The Distinctive Voice: Twentieth Century American Poetry*. Glenview, Illinois, 1966.

Mooney, Stephen. "On Bly's Poetry," *Tennessee Poetry Journal*, II (Winter 1969), 16-18.

Morris, Harry. "A Formal View of the Poetry of Dickey, Garrigue, and Simpson," *Sewanee Review*, LXXVII (April/June 1969), 318-325.

"Notes on People," *New York Times*, Dec. 1, 1971, p. 53.

O'Connor, John J. "Look, Ma, Another Bag of Hot Air," *New York Times*, Sept. 5, 1971, II, p. 11.

"The Poet as Journalist," *Time*, XCII (December 13, 1968), 75.

"Prize Winner," *New York Times Book Review*, March 27, 1966, p. 2.

Shaw, R. B. "Comment," *Poetry*, CXIII (July 1971), 230.

Sloan, Thomas O. "The Open Poem Is a Now Poem: Dickey's May Day Sermon," in *Literature as Revolt and Revolt as Literature: Three Studies in the Rhetoric of Non-Oratorical Forms*. The Proceedings of the Fourth Annual University of Minnesota Spring Symposium in Speech-Communication. Minneapolis, Minnesota, May 3, 1969. pp. 17-31.

Spears, Monroe K. "Poetry Since the Mid-Century," in *Dionysus and the City: Modernism in Twentieth-Century Poetry*. New York: Oxford University Press, 1970.

Taylor, Henry S. "Mr. James Dickey in Orbit" [Poem], *The Sixties*, No. 8 (Spring 1966), 97-98.

Turco, Lewis. "The Suspect in Criticism," *Mad River Review*, I (Spring/Summer 1965), 81-85.

Walsh, Chad, ed. *Today's Poets: American and British Poetry Since the 1930's*. New York, 1964.

"Writers Appeal on Soviet Jews," *New York Times*, May 21, 1967, p. 12.

CONTRIBUTORS

JAMES BOATWRIGHT teaches at Washington and Lee, where he is editor of *Shenandoah.*

RICHARD JAMES CALHOUN is Alumni Professor of English at Clemson University. He is co-editor of *A Tricentennial Anthology of South Carolina Literature* and the author of several essays on contemporary American poets.

PETER DAVISON lives in New York City, where he is the director of the Atlantic Monthly Press. A well known poet, he is the author of *The Breaking of the Day* (1964), *The City and the Island* (1966), and *Pretending To Be Asleep* (1969), and the editor of *Songs of the British Music Hall* (1969).

ARTHUR GREGOR, a native of Vienna, Austria, currently resides in New York City. He is the author of several volumes of poems, including *Basic Movements* (1966), *Figure In the Door* (1968), and *A Bed By the Sea* (1970). His *Selected Poems* appeared in 1971.

ROBERT W. HILL is Assistant Professor of English at

Clemson University. His Ph.D. dissertation at the University of Illinois was on the attitudes toward nature in the poetry of Theodore Roethke and James Dickey.

CAROLYN KIZER is a member of the creative writing staff at the University of North Carolina at Chapel Hill. She is the author of a volume of poetry, *Knock Upon Silence* (1965).

RICHARD KOSTELANETZ is the author of numerous books on contemporary American culture, among them, *The Theatre of Mixed Means* (1968) and *Master Minds* (1969). He is the editor of *The New American Writers* (1967). He lives in New York City.

GEORGE LENSING is a member of the English Department at the University of North Carolina at Chapel Hill, where he specializes in contemporary American literature.

LAURENCE LIEBERMAN is Associate Professor of English at the University of Illinois at Urbana. He is the author of a volume of poems, *The Unblinding* (1968), and the editor of *The Achievement of James Dickey* (1968).

DANIEL B. MARIN has taught creative writing at the University of South Carolina, where he was associated with James Dickey. He is currently at the University of Iowa.

WILLIAM J. MARTZ is Professor of English at Ripon College and author of *The Distinctive Voice* (1966), editor of *The Achievement of Robert Lowell* and *The Achievement of Theodore Roethke* (1966). His most recent work on contemporary American poetry is *John Berryman, University of Minnesota Pamphlets* (1969).

PAUL RAMSEY is Alumni Distinguished Professor of English at the University of Tennessee at Chattanooga. His volumes of poetry include *The Lively and the Just* (1962), *In An Ordinary Place* (1965), and *The Deers* (1968). His critical study, *The Art of John Dryden,* was published by the University of Kentucky Press in 1969.

THOMAS O. SLOAN is Professor of Rhetoric at the University of California at Berkeley. He is co-author of *The Oral Study of Literature* (1966).

H. L. WEATHERBY is Associate Professor of English at Vanderbilt University, where he specializes in Victorian and Modern literature.